Beyond the Growth Dilemma
Toward an
Ecologically Integrated Economy

Quaker Institute for the Future Pamphlet Series

Quaker Institute for the Future Pamphlets aim to provide critical information and understanding born of careful discernment on social, economic, and ecological realities, inspired by the testimonies and values of the Religious Society of Friends (Quakers). We live in a time when social and ecological issues are converging toward catastrophic breakdown. Human adaptation to social, economic and planetary realities must be re-thought and re-designed. *Quaker Institute for the Future Pamphlets* are dedicated to this calling based on a spiritual and ethical commitment to "right relationship" with Earth's whole commonwealth of life.

Quaker Institute for the Future

Beyond the Growth Dilemma Toward an Ecologically Integrated Economy

Edited by
Ed Dreby
Judy Lumb

Quaker Institute for the Future Pamphlet 6
Quaker Institute for the Future 2012

Published for Quaker Institute for the Future by *Producciones de la Hamaca*, Caye Caulker, Belize <producciones-hamaca.com>

ISBN: 978-976-8142-48-1

Beyond the Growth Dilemma: Toward an Ecologically Integrated Economy is the sixth in the series of Quaker Institute for the Future Pamphlets:

Series ISBN: 978-976-8142-21-4

Producciones de la Hamaca is dedicated to:
—Celebration and documentation of Earth
    and all her inhabitants,
—Restoration and conservation of Earth's
    natural resources,
—Creative expression of the sacredness of
    Earth and Spirit.

Contents

v

ACKNOWLEDGEMENTS

It was on my initiative that the Growth Dilemma Project of Philadelphia Yearly Meeting (PYM) collaborated with Quaker Institute for the Future (QIF) to publish this pamphlet, and its companion pamphlet, *It's the Economy, Friends.* So I am taking the liberty of thanking those who have helped to make it possible.

I must first thank our authors, four of whom are active members of the Growth Dilemma Project: Pamela Haines, Clerk; Steve Loughin, Treasurer; J. Tucker Taylor; and David Watkins. We have all put a lot of work into this, and I trust we have all learned in the process. Others active with the Growth Dilemma Project who made important contributions are Burt Dallas, David George, Hollister Knowlton, Margaret Mansfield, and Dan Turner.

I also want to thank Paul Krumm, who wrote about the monetary system, the most controversial of our topics. We made a very difficult decision not to include his chapter because it did not fit well within the space, character, and flow of the whole. But we've asked, and he has agreed, to provide an augmented version of "The Values of Money," to anyone who emails him <pkrumm@rhelectric.net>.

In addition I want to thank Friends from nine yearly meetings who reviewed one or more of the chapters: Betsy Allen, David Bantz, Neal Burdick, Al Connor, Charlie Davis, Barbara Day, Phil Emmi, Tom Head, Bill Upholt, and Vince Zelazny. To this list, I add members of the QIF publications committee: Charlie Blanchard, Gray Cox, Geoffrey Garver, and Shelley Tannenbaum.

The Growth Dilemma Project and its focus on economics and Friends testimonies in an ecological context would not exist without two good Friends, Peter G. Brown and Thomas Swain.

Peter participated in key events at Pendle Hill in 2003, and Haverford College in 2006, and helped to establish QIF. He provided the leadership for QIF's Moral Economy Project that published *Right Relationship: Building a Whole Earth Economy* in 2009. *Right Relationship* provided the theme for our Yearly Meeting's 2009 Annual Session, at which Peter was a plenary speaker.

Thomas Swain, the retiring Clerk of Philadelphia Yearly Meeting, presided at the 2009 Annual Session. In early 2010, those of us charged by the Yearly Meeting to carry its heart-felt but unfocused concern about economics and ecology were uncertain of a way forward. Thomas took the initiative to help organize a major event, from which came direction, allies, and a sense of purpose and possibility.

My closest associates in the preparation of both QIF Pamphlet #5, *It's the Economy, Friends,*" and now #6, *"Beyond the Growth Dilemma,"* have been author and co-author Keith Helmuth, co-editor Judy Lumb, and my wife Margaret Mansfield. Margaret was both an author, co-author, and editor for QIF #5. Ever since we were led almost 20 years ago to discern how we might do something about a deteriorating human-Earth relationship, Margaret and I have either collaborated or assisted one another in everything each of us has done. For this I have been truly blessed.

In 2000, when Keith moved to Philadelphia, we became close colleagues in PYM's Environmental Working Group and its project on Friends Testimonies and Economics. Keith was instrumental in establishing QIF, and as chair of its publications committee, launched the QIF pamphlet series. The first QIF pamphlet, *Fueling Our Future*, was also a collaboration between QIF and Philadelphia Yearly Meeting's Environmental Working Group. After Keith returned to Canada in 2008 we have continued an active partnership. As a co-author of *Right Relationship* he was also a plenary speaker at the 2009 PYM Annual Session, and he has been a *de facto* member of the Growth Dilemma Project ever since.

I first met Judy electronically from Belize, also in the year 2000. Within a short time she began to lead the editorial team of *Quaker Eco-Bulletin* (*QEB*) that included Barbara Day and Sandra Lewis, both of whom I had met at a National Council of Churches Eco-Justice Conference in 1999. Judy and I were Internet colleagues for several years before we actually met in person. While we occasionally see each other in person, Judy, Keith, and I have developed a working friendship over the Internet that has for me, and I think for them, had an important spiritual dimension. For this I am also truly blessed.

QEB has been an important voice for Friends' concerns at the intersection of ecology and economics as they have developed within the wider Quaker community. All past *QEB*s can be found at <quakerearthcare.org>. The most recent *QEB* is a tribute to Sandra Lewis, who passed away just a year ago. The *QEB* editorial team began also editing the QIF pamphlets, so that editorial team now includes Judy Lumb, Barbara Day, and Charles Blanchard. Judy's publishing non-profit in Belize, *Producciones de la Hamaca*, publishes the QIF pamphlets.

I must thank one more person. Kim Carlyle was a partner in many past efforts. He transformed *QEB* from an informal report circulated by e-mail into a legitimate publication, and created a place for *QEB* in the newsletter of Quaker Earthcare Witness (QEW). He had a key role in engaging QEW with the political aspect of seeking "an earth restored." After he left QEW, he desk-top published a resource for Friends Testimonies and Economics called *Seeds of Violence, Seeds of Hope*, from which much of QIF #5 was assembled. Kim has since moved on to other things. I miss him, and I will be forever grateful for the contribution he made to this effort.

Ed Dreby
Co-Editor
October, 2012

CHAPTER ONE

Introduction
The Growth Dilemma Project
Keith Helmuth and Ed Dreby

This generation's Great Work is the transformative effort to change human-Earth relations from disruptive and destructive to mutually enhancing and beneficial. —Thomas Berry[1]

Once we begin to look at earth as a spaceship, the appalling extent of our ignorance about it is almost frightening. . . . Man must be made to realize that all his major problems are still unsolved, and that a very large and massive intellectual effort is still necessary to solve them.
—Kenneth Boulding[2]

There is no elegant solution to a poorly defined problem. —Joe Volk[3]

In 2009 the book, *Right Relationship: Building a Whole Earth Economy,*[4] provided the theme for Philadelphia Yearly Meeting (Religious Society of Friends, Quakers). As a result, the Growth Dilemma Project was charged by the Yearly Meeting with the task of promoting a wider dialogue about the intersection of ecology and the economy. We see this task as an application of the testimony of integrity, one of the basic principles or testimonies of Friends.[5]

Philadelphia Yearly Meeting's book of discipline, *Faith and Practice,* describes integrity as "a wholeness and harmony of the various aspects of one's life, and truthfulness in whatever one says and does."[6] Integrity as wholeness denotes a condition in which the relationships among the parts of a whole help to sustain, restore, and renew the whole. The integration of one's inner and outer selves makes for the wholeness of the self. Similarly, personal integrity characterized by altruism and trust-worthiness helps a group of people create a community of the whole.

How does the testimony on integrity apply to the intersection of ecology and the economy? Why do Friends need to attend to this intersection, not only for the testimony on integrity, but also for the testimonies on peace, equality, community, and stewardship of the environment?

The dilemmas we face about economic growth—as individuals, nations, and a species—can be understood as a striking example of social and biological "dis-integration." Our current economic system lacks integrity. It is failing to establish mutually beneficial relationships among the parts of our society as a whole—its people and communities. And it is failing to establish a viable relationship with the biosphere of which it is a part—Earth's commonwealth of life.

These failures are evident from:

- increasing mal-distribution of education, employment, security, and well-being;
- increasing disruption of climate, soils, other species, and Earth's ecological systems; and
- violence and injustice, within and between nations, associated with this mal-distribution and disruption.

All this is calling into question not only the future well-being of our descendants, but even the survival of life as we know it.

How can Friends and other concerned people attend to our moral and spiritual integrity unless we are aware of, and engaged with, the realities of our social and biophysical environments, and our society's destructive relationship with the commonwealth of life?

Early Friends had a practice of greeting one another by asking, "How does Truth prosper with thee?" To be truthful, we must acknowledge that, although Philadelphia Yearly Meeting has agreed that there are serious problems at the intersection of ecology and the economy, a unified witness has not yet developed.

As in many other religious and secular communities concerned about these problems, it is not easy to agree about why they are happening or what can be done about them. We have yet to invest the time and energy that coming to more corporate unity will require. In spite of all the rhetoric about a sustainable economy and living sustainably, no one knows exactly how a complex economy can function within Earth's bio-capacities, especially at present and expected population levels. Yet, it is easy to see how we are exceeding Earth's bio-physical limits.[7] Therefore, we have good reason to ask what must be done so the economic system can be made to function within these limits.

2

From its inception, the Society of Friends viewed religious experience rather than church dogma as the foundation for its faith and practice. This experiential orientation leads to a core belief in continuing revelation, which in turn leads most Friends to regard the scientific method as a valid way to increase human understanding. As scientific understanding changes, Friends tend to regard these changes as an aspect of God's continuing revelation, and to integrate these changes into their worldview.

We know a good deal about biochemical processes, energy flows, and atmospheric conditions that underwrite organic life, and habitats in which life flourishes.[8] The science of ecology can teach us about how naturally balanced ecosystems function in a steady state. Economies could be molded along the lines of the dynamic relationships that keep Earth's ecosystems flourishing. Economic expansion has direct and obvious effects on ecosystems, and so do extremes of wealth and poverty. These factors contribute to violent conflicts, which in turn cause more damage to ecosystems. Concerns for peace, social justice, and protecting the biosphere are all intertwined, invoking Quaker testimonies of simplicity, peace, community and equality.

If our Quaker witness is to help promote the wider dialogue on the intersection of ecology and the economy, we must begin at home, in our own Yearly Meetings, with other Friends organizations, and especially with Friends Committee on National Legislation (FCNL). How can we seek more unity about the causes of our economic dilemma and the way forward to a better state of health for the human-Earth relationship?

One way is to explore the various perceptions, assumptions, emotions, and values from which our differing orientations derive, as well as the scientific evidence that is available for our guidance. If we take integrity as our guiding principle, we will recognize that our changed ecological circumstances require significant changes in our economy and its institutions.

A wider dialogue is desperately needed to get us beyond the growth dilemma. Toward this end, *Beyond the Growth Dilemma* offers an explanation of what drives our current economic system's expansion. We invite you to consider some ideas and proposals that point in the direction we must go. We describe as best we can a realistic picture of the distance we have to travel and the challenges before us. And we suggest some of the ways that everyone can contribute to moving in the right direction.

3

Chapter Two "The Growth Dilemma" explains the dilemma that we face. Our economic systems have evolved to promote expansion and that economic expansion has already overshot Earth's biocapacity.

The next two chapters describe two orientations to the growth dilemma that are prominent among member of the Religious Society of Friends, and among concerned citizens generally.

Chapter Three "Is Good Growth Possible?" describes the view that good economic growth is essential and possible by reforming the current economic system. If the market system is to work for the common good, prices must reflect the true value and cost of products and services. The current system enables the wealthy to accumulate more wealth at the expense of the middle class and the poor. But still those taking this approach consider government programs that promote social justice, reduce poverty, and protect the environment to be essential, along with economic growth.

Chapter Four "Can Prosperity Continue Without Economic Growth?" describes the view that economic activity already exceeds ecosystem limits to a dangerous extent, so our economy needs to be integrated with Earth's biophysical capacities. However, economic growth is desperately needed in some regions of the world to end poverty. To make room for this economic growth without exacerbating ecological overshoot, there must be a "compassionate retreat" by overdeveloped regions to reduce their impact on Earth.[9]

Clearly these two approaches are not mutually exclusive. Both approaches agree that a loss of socio-economic and ecosystem integrity has occurred, which public policy and legislation is failing to address. There are, however, real differences in assumptions, analysis, and aims that can be brought to further discernment. The intersection of economics and ecology lies within the field of the biophysical sciences, and this scientific perspective provides the best context we have for assessing and relating these two approaches to the human and planetary future.

The next three chapters discuss vital parts of the socio-economic system, and some of the ideas that already exist to move toward a more ecologically integrated economy, whether through ecologically benign growth, or by reducing the net impact of the global economy on Earth's bio-productivity:

- *Chapter Five "Meaningful Jobs and Livelihoods"*
- *Chapter Six "Establishing and Enhancing Responsible Production," and*

- **Chapter Seven *"The Commons, Collaborative Organizations, and New Technologies."***

These topics correspond both to mainstream economists' factors of production—labor, capital, and land, as described in Chapter Three, and to the ecological economists' basic types of capital—social and human, manufactured, and natural, as described in Chapter Eight. The ideas and proposals in Chapters Five, Six, and Seven are inter-related and some are already in play as ways of moving beyond the dilemmas of the current growth economy. Yet their possibilities become more apparent if seen as parts of a whole rather than as isolated changes.

Chapter Eight "An Ecologically Integrated Economy" describes a framework drawn from the ideas of Kenneth Boulding,[10] Herman Daly,[11] and others, for how a complex economy might be managed to function within Earth's bio-capacities. This chapter also points to the greater challenge of cultural change that would be needed to support an ecologically integrated economy.

Chapter Nine "The Way Forward" describes ways everyone can help to move our current economy toward one that is more ecologically integrated. A series of questions provide policy guidance to assess specific legislative and policy proposals to determine if they might move us in the directions we need to go.

There is a tendency to blame our societal problems on moral failings in general, or evil people in particular: greedy corporate executives, misguided and corrupt politicians, and addicted consumers. Yet not long ago, Thomas Berry warned against this, saying that there will always be evil people, but our problems exist because so many capable people are doing an excellent job of what they are expected to do.[12] The growth dilemma has arisen because our society has been very successful in doing what seemed like the right thing economically, but which, in many instances, has turned out to be the wrong thing for the integrity of our communities and Earth's life support system.

Blaming moral failings or human nature is a barrier to considering how values and behavior are shaped by culture in which the economic system's institutions and incentives are a major factor. Corporations blame market competition and consumer demand for the damage they cause. Economists blame politicians for the negative effects of bad economic policy. Population biologists blame ever-increasing human numbers for the bad effects of over-development. Environmentalists blame the government for failure to enact adequate environmental regulations.

Although there may be plenty of blame to go around, focusing on blame offers little resolution for this exceedingly complex problem. We need to attend to the systemic failings—economic, political, and cultural—that have created this impasse. We hope that relating the Quaker testimony on integrity to the need for a whole system perspective, along with these practical proposals, will be engaging and energizing for Friends and others. We believe that bringing this perspective and these questions to the forefront of an ongoing conversation with policy-makers would constitute an important Quaker witness on ecology and the economy, and be a valuable role for the Society of Friends.

CHAPTER TWO
The Growth Dilemma
Ed Dreby and Keith Helmuth

In the 1960s, Quaker economist Kenneth Boulding warned that humanity would soon be challenged to make a transition from a "cowboy economy" that assumes there are limitless resources to a "spaceship economy" that is bound by the realities of biology and physics on a finite planet. Will humanity, he asked, choose to use Earth's limited supplies of non-renewable resources for developing an economy and society that could use renewable resources to function indefinitely as part of Earth's self-renewing biophysical system?[13]

Ecological Footprint Analysis shows that globally we are using approximately one and a half times Earth's biocapacity to renew resources and absorb pollution. The U.S. uses four times its biocapacity.[14] This overshoot results in depletion of fisheries, forests, fresh water, and an accumulation of greenhouse gases and other pollution. In addition to this reduction of ecosystems services, the Millennium Ecosystem Assessment shows an incredible loss of biodiversity. Extinctions are happening now at one thousand times the rate in the fossil records.[15]

Whether mindful people place their hopes on redirecting economic growth or on enabling economies to prosper without expanding, our nation continues to squander its time and resources, and increasingly invests in denial. As a global society, we do not yet realize that our survival depends on functioning within the limits of Earth's regenerative capacities. When this realization truly takes hold, we will need to restructure our economies so our societies can thrive while the use of physical resources decreases rather than increases.[16]

What Drives the Current System's Expansion?

Three elements in the current system drive its expansion:

1) expanding populations of people, machines, and money (*shown in the following graph*),
2) uses of surplus, and
3) our banking and financial system.

7

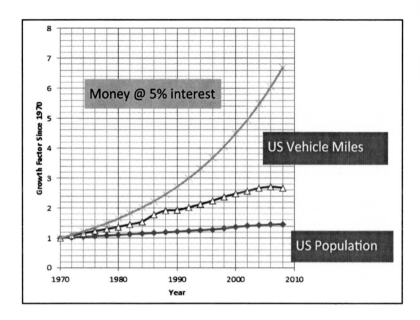

Human population growth is a major problem. We are told that after the current demographic bulge, reducing child mortality and improving women's educational and economic opportunities will solve the problem. Yet no one knows if this will happen, or if less desirable circumstances will intervene until the population actually stops increasing. Yet human numbers are not the most immediate problem.

Burgeoning populations of manufactured capital, such as, vehicles, buildings, roads, bridges, airports, and malls, are depleting resources and disrupting ecosystems. In order to pay for them, we must use the machines and buildings we make and that takes energy. So we risk environmental catastrophe to drill for oil, frack for gas, move mountains for coal, and get fuel from tar sands. If we truly want to reduce pollution, we will have to reduce our populations of manufactured capital, particularly those that must be fed fossil fuels to live useful lives.

From 1970 to 2007 the global money supply grew from about $2 trillion to about $60 trillion. More money is something that almost everyone wants, so few people view this increase as a problem. However, money's value hinges on being able to exchange it for goods and services. If the supply of money increases faster than the supply of goods and services that people with money want, the value of money will suffer and prices of everything will go up.

8

As long as the human population keeps growing, so will the demand for food, clothing, shelter, healthcare and education. In recent years, it has only been possible to fill this demand by expanding financial markets and inventing new financial products.

But most of this new money is not used for basic needs of growing populations. Rather, it is used to make even more money for those who are already wealthy, and to promote unneeded and often frivolous consumption by those who already have much more than they need or even truly want. Many people are heavily in debt from excessive consumption. An increasing number are borrowing to pay for basic needs, while others join the growing numbers of working poor, under-employed, and unemployed.

The Role of Economic Surplus

In hunter-gatherer cultures, people tended to use only as much time as necessary to provide for their physical needs. They used their surplus time for community activities of various kinds. This is one reason that it took millennia for technologies to change. The creation of economic surplus seems to have occurred when an elite class developed and acquired enough influence to exploit the labor of those with less influence in a systematic way. Economic development occurred when the surplus of the elite was used to produce more and better things. The invention of money to accumulate value and facilitate exchange was an important factor in promoting economic development.

The flow of economic activity and money between businesses and households is basic to the functioning of a market economy. If households have a surplus and choose to save some of their income, that money is withheld from circulation. When this happens, not enough money will be spent to pay for what businesses produce and the level of activity will not be sustained unless the savings are restored to circulation.

As a household's income increases, so does its propensity to save. The system then has to create both more incentives to spend and more ways to return savings to the circular flow. When income differentials become extreme, as is now the case, developing enough new ways to use the savings of the very wealthy becomes problematic because their investments make them even wealthier which compounds the problem.[8]

Money, Banking, and Finance

In our current economic system, household savings are returned to the circular flow of economic activity through the banking and financial system, primarily when banks make loans. This is also how most of the money supply is created.

Banks are required to hold only a fraction of their deposits as liquid reserves to cover cash withdrawals, usually about five percent. This enables banks to make loans of up to 20 times their reserves, and sometimes even more.

More than 95% of today's money supply exists as credit balances in bank accounts that enable borrowers to spend money the banks create by making loans. This is how most new money is created, and how the money supply is expanded. It means the banking system has a multiplier effect on the money supply, but also a reverse multiplier effect if banks decrease their lending.

The rest of the money supply is created when the Federal Reserve Bank (the Fed) lends money to the U.S. government; i.e., by buying government debt. Since borrowers pay interest to banks, and the government pays interest on its debt, virtually the entire money supply is created by debt, and interest is being paid on every dollar that debt creates. Debt plus interest is greater than the credit that loans create. If the economy is expanding because of abundant resources and new markets, an expanding money supply can enable both creditors and debtors to prosper. But if expansion slows, some debtors will be forced to default on their loans, banks will reduce their lending, and a contracting money supply will lead to recession.[17]

Since the 1970s, banking deregulation, coupled with electronic technologies, has made it easier for banks to lend, and thus to greatly increase the money supply, level of debt, and size of financial markets in relation to the real economy of goods and services.[18] The Financial Services Act of 1999 permitted integration of banking and financial systems, which allowed new financial practices like mortgaged-backed securities and credit-default swaps. This facilitated further expansion of the financial economy until the collapse of the financial markets in 2008 created the Great Recession.[19]

The Fed can influence banks to make loans, especially in good times, but it can't compel banks to make loans in bad times. Although our dollar bills are Federal Reserve Notes, if banks won't lend, the only way the Fed is supposed to increase the money supply directly is to buy more debt from the government. The only way the government can increase the money supply directly is to sell more debt to the Fed. This is why the government is apt to become the borrower of last resort to prevent a depression.

Thus, virtually the entire money supply comes from debt on which interest must be paid. While the national debt, i.e., the debt of the federal government, receives a lot of attention, corporate and household debt is much larger than the national debt. In order to sustain current levels of debt and prevent a reverse multiplier effect, great efforts are made to promote consumer spending and private sector investment. As the accumulation of debt drives economic expansion, the incentives increase to exploit land and labor in the real economy; and so do the incentives to make money from speculation in financial markets rather than by producing anything of real value.[20]

There is a stark contrast between the views of traditional economists and ecological economists about the role of money and finance in the economy. Traditional economic theory views money as an ethically neutral facilitator of economic activity. It holds that in a properly functioning economy, the relationship between economic activity and the supply of money will be self-regulating, and the role of government is to help the economy function properly. The proponents of this theory who are troubled by the economy's failures think the system's regulatory regime needs to be restored and modernized to deal with new technologies and to end the abuses these technologies have spawned.

This view is challenged by ecological economists who assert that these economic systems evolved at a time when the resources of Earth seemed unlimited, but that situation has changed dramatically. Now our economic systems have become so large and ecologically damaging that they must be fundamentally changed to establish mutually beneficial relationships with their host ecosystems. Because endless economic expansion on a finite planet is impossible, and because our current monetary and financial systems are apt to become unstable unless the economy is expanding, ecological economists think that the monetary system must be fundamentally reformed.

We need our monetary and financial systems to help facilitate the establishment of an ecologically integrated economy, rather than to intensify, as is now happening, the dis-integration between our economy and our society's social and ecological imperatives. There is much that must be done to redirect humanity's economic activities to function with fewer physical resources and less ecologically damaging effects. This will require attending to the troubled relationship between our system of money and finance, and our economic system as a whole.

11

CHAPTER THREE

Is Good Growth Possible?
J. Tucker Taylor

The fundamental economic problem is how to provide for the material well-being of society. To do so, any society must cope with a number of questions. What goods and services will be produced, and in what quantities? How are those goods and services to be produced? For whom is the resulting output produced, *i.e.* who gets what shares of the economic pie? How much land, labor, and capital are used? How can society adapt to change? Over the millennia, human societies have devised three broad ways to answer these questions, three "types" of socio-economies: 1) tradition, 2) deliberate planning or direction, and 3) the market.

Tradition, of course, is the oldest. Planning seems the most rational. We in capitalist economies often conceive any deliberate social planning as totalitarian or dictatorial, but of course it is not so. In fact, we turn over many major economic decisions to democratically chosen bodies, school boards, the Social Security Administration, the Environmental Protection Agency. The third approach, the market, leaves it up to individuals, as producers and consumers, as workers, or as lenders and borrowers, to pursue their own interests. Adam Smith argued that such a system would eventually evolve into one driven, "as if by an invisible hand," to provide income and output for all.

No actual society ever has functioned purely according to tradition, planning, or the market. Capitalism, for example, has tremendous variety. There is Dickensian London, the dark satanic mills, the horrendous coal and iron mines, knitting mills and their child laborers. But there is also Scandinavia, the great Middle Way, a kinder, gentler capitalism, a socialized capitalism.

The great 40-year period in the U.S. extending from the 1930s to the 1970s witnessed the blossoming of the modern American middle class via a hundred subtle channels: beginnings of minimum wages; huge government purchases of goods and services like the Interstate Highway System (and sadly, military goods) with accompanying employment at decent wages and working conditions; a very progressive income tax (once with 90% marginal tax rates); benefits of the post-World War II GI bill—college education and mortgages; and the establishment of a minimal safety net of Social Security, Unemployment Insurance, Workers' Compensation, Food Stamps, Housing Assistance, Medicare, and Aid to Families with Dependent Children (now Temporary Assistance to Needy Families). There was a distinct lessening of the inequalities in income and to some extent in wealth. The poorest 20 percent of the population went from sharing three to four percent of the Gross Domestic Product (GDP) in the 1920s to six percent by the 1970s with the share of the richest 20 percent decreasing from more than 50 percent to 47 percent.

The middle class bought houses and middle class children went to college. Firms instituted pension plans. The result was that getting old no longer meant getting poor. Those over 65 years went from having a larger fraction of their age cohort in poverty to having a smaller-than-national-average percentage in poverty by the 1970s. Workplace safety improved. Unions protected a larger fraction of the labor force. Median income doubled and then doubled again. By the 1970s, working middle class families were buying vacation homes and taking trips to Europe.

Our current angst, a broad but vague and inarticulate uneasiness might be traced to the reversal of many of these trends beginning in the mid-1970s and accelerating in the 1990s into the new millennium. The century-long annual increase in GDP per capita has continued, but whereas in the 1932-1975 period it was widely shared, since then the fruits of the continuing growth have accrued almost entirely to the rich, and in the last 15 years to the very rich. Income and wealth inequalities in the U.S. have reverted to the levels of the 1930s, as is shown in the graph below of the income share of the top ten percent in the U.S.[21]

13

What Generated the Good Growth Era
of the 1930s to 1970s?

In 1936 John Maynard Keynes explained the business cycle, the recurring boom and bust. It has turned out that capitalism has a sort of breathing rhythm, a few years of expanding output followed by a few years of contracting output. For a few years, propelled sometimes by a new invention or fad or burst of optimism, business firms erect office buildings, new houses and apartments, factories, shopping malls. Then at some monthly executive committee meeting a board member says, "Maybe we had better slow down just a tad, open say one new store every 2 months instead of every month." When such decisions are reached in several different industries simultaneously, the boom has peaked, the crash comes, and a period of contraction begins, with the accompanying slowing of inflation (in extreme cases deflation), and snowballing unemployment.

Keynes said that if the total demand for goods and services collapsed because business firms stopped building houses and consumers stopped buying automobiles and furniture, then another purchaser of the nation's output, the government, would have to step in and pick up the slack. It was the intellectual underpinning for what governments were already doing under pressure from the people. Governments started to spend on public works projects, and hired millions of mostly young men. In the U.S. they built Fairmount Park in Philadelphia, Skyline Drive, Hoover Dam, and the San Francisco Bay Bridge. They built schools; they wrote and produced plays; they strung electric and telephone wires across the country; and they made it possible to drive all the way from New York to Los Angeles on paved roads. The investment has been repaid a hundred-fold.

What Changed in the 1970s?

It is a sad fact that a counterrevolution was mounted to discredit Keynes and the fiscal policy that can shorten and dampen the business cycle. The beginning of this counterrevolution has been pinpointed to a memo written by Lewis Powell to the U.S. Chamber of Commerce on August 23, 1971, two months before he was nominated to the Supreme Court. The long memo, over 6,000 words, strongly urged a counterattack against these leavening influences of the previous 40 years. The memo was leaked to columnist Jack Anderson, who used it to try to discredit Powell's objectivity in the confirmation process, but he was confirmed and served as a moderate influence on the Supreme Court from 1972 to 1987. The Chamber of Commerce took Powell's advice to heart and a number of organizations were formed to try to shape public opinion toward free-market capitalism without regulation. Some of the regulations that had been instituted after the Great Depression were rolled back.[22]

GDP and Growth

GDP, that dollar figure that is now about $50,000 per person per year in the U.S., is composed of:

- The value of the goods and services people consume (food, clothing, heart transplants, trips to Disneyland);

- The value of the capital goods that business firms purchase or build (fork-lift trucks, computers, drill presses, power plants, shopping malls, casinos, rent-a-cars);

- The value of the goods and services that governments use to fulfill their public commitments (services of the police, firemen, trash collectors, street sweepers, schoolteachers, and the purchase of police cars, fire trucks, school buses, tanks, jeeps, aircraft carriers and battleships); and

- The goods and services we sell to our foreign trading partners (aircraft to the world's airlines, medical and scientific equipment, agricultural products, entertainment) minus the things they sell us (French wine, autos, clothing, trips to Machu Pichu).

Such a variety of goods and services make up the GDP that it is quite possible to envision "clean and green" growth of GDP; concentrated in the future, no doubt, on relatively environmentally friendly services rather than glass and steel and other hard resource-rich goods; and there is no obvious limit to clean and green growth.

The GDP per worker can increase through three mechanisms:

- An increase in the physical capital per worker,

- An increase in knowledge, or human capital, per worker, and

- An improvement in the state-of-the-art technology

An economy's resource base, the stock of resources or the raw materials that go into producing our food, clothing, houses and tools for further production can be grouped into three categories: land, labor, and capital.

15

Land

In economic analysis land means not only square feet of arable farm land; it also encompasses all the sites suitable for industrial or commercial use, all the ores and minerals buried in Earth, trees in the forest, fish in the sea, and sites suitable for waste disposal; all the naturally occurring, economically useful parts of the planet, including the planet's capacity to absorb damage, dissipate bad by-products, and rejuvenate itself.

Labor

Labor means human brain and muscle power. It is usually restricted to relatively unskilled labor, only those skills of a young person embarking on a working life with a basic high school education (the ability to read, write, and do arithmetic). Acquired skills like typing or bricklaying come under capital.

Capital

Capital is the accumulated total of all the human-made aids to production. It is of two types, physical capital (the tools) and human capital (our accumulated knowledge), such as, crop rotation or terracing.

Physical capital includes not only steel mills, electric power plants, oil refineries, and gas pipelines; it also includes:

- Office buildings, shopping malls, hotels, apartment buildings and houses,

- Paved roads, railroad tracks, airport runways, ship channels, and seaports,

- Government and university research labs,

- Elementary, high school and college facilities, and educational equipment,

- Hospitals, doctor and dentist offices, and pharmacies,

- Museums, libraries, courthouses, jails, and

- Public parks, swimming pools, tennis courts, and bike paths.

Some of this physical capital comes into being because private investors thought they could make a profit from it. So they borrowed money and invested, that is, purchased or caused it to be manufactured or built. But quite a large fraction of the physical capital of the U.S. has been the result of public investment by government, not private enterprise. In the list above the office buildings and shopping malls were the result of private profit-seeking investment. But the roads, bridges, schools and universities, and sewer lines are all from public, not private, investment. The airplanes were purchased by the airlines, but the airport, runways, and control towers were built by public investment.

Human capital, the stock of human knowledge, is partly accumulated in our brain and muscle memories—how to type, lay brick, manipulate spreadsheets, or do a cataract operation. Human capital is also accumulated in storehouses of knowledge—genome maps, dictionaries, encyclopedias, maps. As our health improves through the decades, the stock of human capital rises. Life expectancy increases. Workers circa 1900 were frequently stricken with dysentery, malaria, and other ailments making them unable to work. A century later workers are able to accomplish more foot-pounds of work per week than their great-great grandparents. As this human capital stock accumulates, labor gets more productive per hour of exertion just as with more or better tools.

Technological Progress

In addition to growth in physical and human capital, a third source of increased productivity per hour of effort is technological progress. Some technological progress comes from mechanical improvements—standardized, interchangeable parts or newer-generations of machines requiring less maintenance. And some technological progress is cultural—discovering that workers are more productive if they have better lighting, heating and cooling in the workplace, if they have more stimulating and varied, less monotonous and drudgery-filled work rhythms, and if their contributions to the suggestion box are really valued.

Production Possibility Frontier

To see how economic growth can be "clean and green" nearly as easily as "dirty and brown," we use an analytic device called a "Production Possibility Frontier (PPF)," a graphic presentation of maximum output of goods from a given set of inputs.[23] Let us assume the production of only two goods, bread and tractors, metaphors for consumer goods generally and capital goods generally. We assume an initial endowment of resources and current state-of-the-art of technology, where land also includes all the natural resources required and tractors include all the machines, structures, and knowledge needed.

Land.........................   1,000 acre-equivalents

Labor.........................   10,000 person-days

Capital.........................   100 tractors-equivalents

Each of the curves below are for different levels of input resources and the points on the curve indicate choices made between the two products, bread or tractors.

With the existing stocks of land, labor and capital, the society could produce annually about six and a half million loaves of bread and no tractors, or ten thousand tractor-equivalents and no bread, or various other combinations lying on the solid, curved line. A society that was

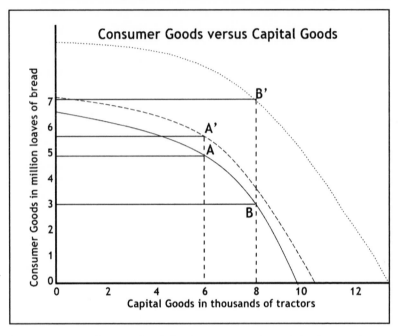

Consumer Goods versus Capital Goods

bent on economic growth might choose to produce eight thousand tractors and three million loaves of bread (point B). A society not so desperate for growth, but more eager for goods to consume this year might choose five million loaves of breads and six thousand tractors (point A).

The world's developing economies find themselves at point A producing five million loaves of bread and six thousand tractors. They now have 100 thousand tractors, but the tractor stock is deteriorating at a rate of five thousand per year. Moreover, the five million loaves of bread is just enough to provide everyone 1800 calories a day of nutrition. However, it takes 2000 calories per day to stay healthy, so they are slowly starving to death. Worse still, they will be adding only one thousand tractors per year. This means that next year's PPF curve will shift out slightly to the dashed curve because the resource base will then be 1000 acres, 10,000 people, and 101 tractors.

The next year they will be able to produce combination A', that is, they will be climbing out of poverty very, very slowly, and only if their population growth is minimal.

Their only hope for a better life for their children and grandchildren is to move this year on the first PPF (solid curve) toward point B, producing eight thousand tractors for a net addition to the capital stock of three thousand for next year. Then the PPF curve shifts beyond the dashed curve to the outermost PPF dotted curve where they can now produce combination B'. However, there is a horrible price. Only three million loaves of bread could be produced this year, which is starving this year's or this generation's people to death even faster—a grim prospect, indeed. But there are some mitigating circumstances. Foreign aid would help and so would technological progress and slower population growth. Perhaps they could specialize in tractor production, exporting them, and buying more bread than could be domestically produced.

From 1920-1980 the Soviet Union chose the B combination of four million loaves of bread and eight thousand tractors, or maybe even two million loaves of bread and nine thousand tractors. That choice pulled the nation into the 20th century with rapid and sustained growth, shifting the PPF curve outward, decade after decade. By the 1970s, however, the people were getting less and less happy with the posters of proud, sweaty workers with rolled-up sleeves and new steel mills. They watched Western Europe on television enjoy a cornucopia of consumer goods (here, metaphorically, bread) and communicated to their leaders: "Enough already with the tractors (and steel mills and power plants). We want to move along the frontier toward more consumer goods (bread); we want automobiles for ourselves," perhaps even realizing that such a choice means slower economic growth in the future.

Further, the PPF curve can be used to compare production in the private sector with that of the public sector (*Curves on p. 20*). Goods and services produced by the private sector on the vertical axis include, besides much that is good, a host of unnecessary, wasteful, tasteless, extravagant, gaudy, sinful, energy-intensive, goods and services. On the horizontal axis is a set of public goods and services for the common good: government-provided health care, public education, mass transit, beautified parks and public spaces, and new rules and laws for jobs that are less dangerous and more fulfilling—all things that collectively assist in raising the level of the life experience for all God's children.

The inner curve represents our current PPF. To move toward more stuff on the horizontal axis, we must sacrifice some of the stuff on the

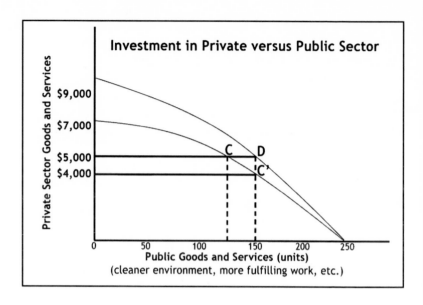

Investment in Private versus Public Sector

Private Sector Goods and Services

$9,000
$7,000
$5,000
$4,000

0   50   100   150   200   250

Public Goods and Services (units)
(cleaner environment, more fulfilling work, etc.)

vertical axis, moving from point C to point C'. Thus, to have more Social Security and a cleaned-up environment and the rest, requires increased taxes to pay for those things, which means less disposable income to buy 52-inch television sets and other toys.

Eonomic growth is possible, through public and private investment, which generates an increase in capital that shifts the PPF outward. It is pictured here as an increase in the potential production of private sector consumer goods on the vertical axis only. There may be no comparable increase in productivity of teachers or caregivers or the available environmental resources such as fresh water on horizontal axis, so the curve shifts outward on every point except the point on the horizontal axis.

But moving to the enlarged or expanded PPF, with economic growth we could have more care in the nursing homes for our grandparents or a cleaner environment with no sacrifice of our current standard of living measured as the privately produced food, clothing, autos, houses and toys, that is, we can move from point C to point D, not just from C to C'. This is the great promise of economic growth. There are many paths to economic growth, not all involving more environmental assault.

20

Current Problems

European and American countries have not had actual growth policies. There have been particular projects that were justified on the basis of spurring or assisting growth, such as dams and shipping canals. Aid to math and science education in the 1950s was justified in the "beat-the-Soviets" Cold War. The interstate highway system was sold as necessary for national defense, though the Interstates shave millions of dollars off corporations' transportation costs, and so further growth.

Because we have not had a pro-growth policy, we do not need a no-growth policy. Our Quaker testimony of Simplicity stands today as it has for 300 years as a pillar of our faith and needs only constant re-interpreting as way opens. We need not oppose economic growth *per se,* nor need we embrace it as a cure-all. What we need is kinder, gentler growth, with attention paid to the pressing social problems of our time, which include:

- Excessive control by giant, transnational corporations;

- Worsening income and wealth distributions;

- Unfair and unsustainable tax structures;

- Drudgery-filled work;

- Excessive advertising that promotes consumption in general;

- Global warming, a looming disaster;

- Bigger, more intimately probing government;

- Rising expectations for government functioning;

- High and persistent unemployment;

- Environmental degradation;

- Deteriorating safety net: cash welfare payments have all but disappeared and Social Security is being challenged;

- Too large a proportion of our citizenry is incarcerated;

- Too many cars, too little mass transit;

- Too many one-acre lots with fenced-in yards, tennis courts and swimming pools instead of public parks with gardens, lakes, and swimming pools;

- Individual health savings accounts instead of national health care;

- Personal savings for retirement instead of expanded Social Security;
- Private and personal weight-reducing diets instead of a public health strategy;
- Too much emphasis on the private, personal, and single family welfare, and not enough emphasis on our shared welfare and fate; and
- Privatization of education, health care, prisons, police, and courts.

Solutions

Make the prices of things reflect their true cost

Production and consumption of many goods causes much harm, but these external costs get sloughed off onto third parties. For example, the full cost of burning coal must take into consideration all the costs of mining and burning. The costs of getting the coal out of the ground might be $50 per ton. But miners get black lung disease and other respiratory ailments; the medical costs might be an additional $10 per ton.

Mining pollutes the nearby streams, reducing fishing livelihoods and recreation opportunities, another $5 per ton. Houses nearby have to be painted more often, another $5 per ton. Local real estate values are half the value of similar houses out of sight and smell of the mine. Those millions of dollars would add another $10 per ton to the cost of coal.

If EPA insists that technologies be developed that would avoid all these spillover effects, the coal mine operators might say, "that would send the price of coal to $80 a ton!" Oil does in fact cost $80 per ton right now; but $30 of it is dispersed among the miners' lungs, the residents' medical insurance premiums, real estate values, etc.

And this is only the production costs. There are also the pollution costs of transporting and burning coal, which creates poor air quality and climate change. Passing stricter environmental protection laws is another way to internalize currently external costs. The production of the offending goods could be taxed, and the tax revenue used to clean up the damage. Another approach is to sell emissions permits that can be traded and the proceeds used to repair the damage. All of these external costs should be internalized and connected to the appropriate goods and services.

Raise the minimum wage

Doubling the minimum wage to $15.00 per hour would permit two working adults to raise a family in a minimally dignified lifestyle. The cry immediately arises that many small firms that are operating on the edge of survival would find it impossible to raise prices sufficient to cover the increased production costs. But that is nonsense. A single firm when confronted with increased costs cannot raise prices, but when all firms in an industry or sector are confronted with the same issues, they can and do raise prices. Those firms that do not raise prices will go out of business, and so they should. There would be a period of upset, turmoil, and repositioning, but that is how the market is supposed to work. Housecleaning services would have to raise prices. The McBurgers on the dollar menu would have to go to two dollars. Buyers of these goods and services would grumble, but they would pay.

Institute a massive public works program

A work program modeled on the 1930s Public Works Administration, Works Projects Administration and Civilian Conservation Corps, would guarantee a job yo every person who wants one. Such employer-of-last-resort policies have been proposed by a number of economists, who stress that this would not be a make-work program of pretend jobs, a thinly veiled income handout. There are any number of urgent public sector tasks that need to be undertaken: repair of our aging and crumbling infrastructure, clean-up of toxic waste sites, proper care for our nursing-home-bound elderly, clean up of our inner cities. The benefits of full employment would be so huge and so pervasive that it is hard to overstate them. For example, during World War II, millions migrated from the South into the northern cities and went to work in the military plants, where they were trained. They had steady jobs at good wages with benefits. Many learned to read and qualified for mortgages for the first time in their family's history. They were transformed from a peasantry into a unionized working class. Other benefits of full employment include:

- Higher wages throughout the economy put a brake on inflationary pressures,
- Increases in potential home buyers as marginally attached labor force participants become persons with steady jobs over a number of years,
- Reduction in street crime, and
- As firms found their wage costs rising, they might be forced to economize on advertising and executive salaries.

Increase the progressivity of the tax structure

Attacking the grossly unequal income and wealth distributions can be done with tax policy, restoring the 60 to 70 percent and higher marginal tax rates of the 1930s and 1940s. Reinstituting stiff estate taxes will make each generation start out on a more nearly level playing field.

Increase Social Security taxes

There are ways to increase Social Security (SS) taxes and benefits progressively. More people are depending on SS for half or more of their retirement income as private company pensions are disappearing. Increase Medicare and Medicaid benefits and figure out how to rein in costs as doctors, hospitals, and pharmaceutical corporations make large profits.

Reduce the numbers in prison

Use community-based treatment and job-training programs to bring many of the prisoners back to being productive members of society.

Elect politicians who will restore our sense of common-ness, "our-ness"

Politicians need to be talking to us about building a common future, not 300,000,000 individual futures.

Establish stricter controls on all advertising

Allowable minutes per hour of TV advertising were increased from 12 to 15 minutes per hour in the 1980s. Let's roll them back. Billboards are not permitted on some highways. Let's try to broaden that ban.

Reinvigorate the Justice Department's anti-trust division

Let there be a presumption that small is beautiful. Resist mergers and conglomerates, unless clear cost savings can be demonstrated. Break up some of the biggest firms. There should be a general strengthening of the clout of all the regulatory agencies, from the Federal Trade Commission and the Securities and Exchange Commission to the Environmental Protection Agency, Occupational Safety and Health Administration, and a dozen others. We need more regulation, not less.

Ban corporate contributions to political campaigns

Our politicians have become dependent on large campaign contributions, and are inevitably corrupted by them. The government must be retrieved for the public purpose. It is truly our only hope.

CHAPTER FOUR
Can Prosperity Continue Without Economic Growth?
Keith Helmuth

What is Happening to the Industrial-Consumer Economy?

When the intersection of economics and ecology is brought into full view, two primary factors stand out; social inequity and ecological degradation. The quest for a moral economy arises from the concern for fairness and justice. The quest for ecological integrity arises from the concern for the health of the commonwealth of life.

Economic growth has certainly been a boon to the convenience and longevity of some of the people who live in the areas where it has flourished, but dire poverty and extreme inequality are now resurgent in these same areas. Growth is certainly needed in areas of the world where major populations have not yet benefitted from even the most basic technologies and economic practices that make for a dignified and secure way of life. In the midst of incredible wealth, adequate access to the means of life is a growing crisis for an increasing number of people.

As the movements for social justice and ecological integrity have come together, those involved have realized that there will be no sustainable progress in eliminating poverty and reducing inequality if the degradation of Earth's ecosystems continues on the course that has been set by the industrial-consumer economy as it now operates. On the one hand, our society and the global economy seem to need constant economic growth; on the other hand, constant economic growth is now undermining the integrity of the ecological conditions that are required for human societies and economies to function effectively and equitably.

This growth dilemma was clearly recognized and fully articulated in the 1960s and early 1970s by a series of prescient biologists and economists. Had ameliorative and precautionary action been taken by government and industry at that time, local, regional, and global

25

economies might now be operating at a high level of steady-state resilience. However, aside from regulations to control pollution, public policy did nothing effective to re-orient economies within a sustainable ecosystem and energy context. We are now in a situation in which the dilemma is acute. Certain consequences seem likely to unfold that are beyond effective management or mitigation.[24]

The economic growth we have been enjoying now appears, more and more, to have been based on a short-sighted and faulty reading of our ecological situation. The consequences of this error are now coming into play, and can be seen at a fundamental level in the energy analysis of biophysical economics. This chapter presents a view of the ecology-economics intersection and offers a few pointers on how we might achieve a new kind of measured prosperity as the fossil fuel era comes to an end.

The Energy Base of Economic Growth

Behind the impasse of economic growth lies the relationship of energy and economics. This impasse is addressed from the ecological side by the discipline of biophysical economics, which goes to the heart of the matter regarding the energy basis of economic activity and human adaptation. Economies expand according to the availability of a dominant energy source, and they contract when that source becomes depleted to the point that energy return on energy invested no longer yields a net benefit to society. We are in big trouble with the economy just now because we have not paid careful attention to the energy factor that is the foundation of economic activity.

Charles Hall argues that our industrial-commercial economy is following the same trajectory in relation to oil that other economic eras have followed in relation to their energy sources.[25] He shows how the oil era started out with a high ratio of Energy Return on Energy Invested (EROEI), approximately 100:1 in the early days of the Texas oil boom. As the easy access oil has been depleted and deeper, more difficult extraction is required, this ratio has dropped steadily all over the world in recent years. By 2006 it had dropped to 19:1. Hall and Klitgaard say that as oil extraction moves further into increasingly difficult zones of access, the EROEI ratio will drop precipitously. When it reaches 3:1, the game is up and the collapse of oil-dependent economic activity will occur.[26]

There is no replacement fuel for oil in the amount required, so economic descent is coming and may have already begun.[27] At the same time, worldwide demand for oil is still increasing and now has a doubling time of 37 years. This is an impossible situation, which is why the U.S. Navy is retrofitting aircraft carriers and jet fighters to run on biofuels. They know the jig is up with petroleum and they aim to keep running as the oil era comes to a highly contested end.[28]

Hall advises that this is not a trap from which we will escape by means of technology, or by adjusting the economy away from material and energy throughput toward services and culture. Nor will the current temporary surge in natural gas and unconventional oil extraction do anything more than slightly delay the inevitable descent. The discontinuity between the current structure and function of the industrial-commercial system and its energy base will become so vast, and so fast moving, that no patching up of a technical fix can forestall a major decline of economies that have been built on low cost oil.[29]

The Compounding Role of Climate Change

The oil depletion scenario has generally been thought of as switching to renewable energy in time to keep the industrial-commercial economy functioning without major disruption. It has been assumed that we can keep using oil as long as it lasts, and the more we continue to find, the longer we have to make the switch.

But a very large part of the fossil fuel deposits that are still in the ground must be left in the ground if Earth's climate is to stabilize in a temperature range that allows human settlement to continue within its present tropical and mid-latitude geographic zones.[30] Private and state-owned energy companies have fossil fuel sources on their books that, if burned, represent the equivalent of 2,795 gigatons of carbon dioxide added to the atmosphere. Current calculations estimate that no more than 565 gigatons of carbon dioxide can be released over the next 50 years without breaching a two-degree-Celsius increase. Climate scientists consider that if the temperature increase is kept below two degrees C, some semblance of human civilization can survive.[31]

There are now small signs that attitudes toward fossil fuels are changing. For example, in 2010 President Correa of Ecuador signed the Yasuni ITT initiative to prohibit the extraction of 850 million barrels of oil from the area under Yasuni National Park, which prevents 410 million metric tons of carbon dioxide from entering the atmosphere.[32] This bold political action is unprecedented, but hopefully a harbinger of things to come. Oil dependent economies will further subside as the realization dawns that burning all Earth's fossil fuels threatens the survival of civilization.

27

The Collapse of Complex Societies

Joseph Tainter's research into the failures of complex societies throughout history shows a pattern of remarkable consistency. Complex societies fail when the level of resources devoted to maintaining their complexity is so great that almost no margin remains for dealing with unexpected trauma, shock, or stress. At that point, even a seemingly minor challenge, poorly addressed, may become a tipping point toward collapse. Some societal collapses are sudden and some protracted. The common factor is a growth in complexity that requires a high percentage of social, economic, and environmental resources just for maintenance, leaving little for responding to crisis or creatively adapting to new circumstances. The high cost of complexity militates against resilience and ramps up the level of risk with which a society is required to live.[33]

Ulrich Beck has described the contemporary situation of complex "super-industrialism" as having created "the world risk society."[34] Beck observes that human adaptation has moved from being concerned primarily with natural hazards to now dealing continuously with manufactured hazards, hazards that appear as a result of the pursuit of economic growth and the decision making associated with this quest. With the advent of chemical, hydro-carbon, nuclear, genetic, and nano-technologies, the ecological and social context of manufactured risk has become total. According to Beck, the risks introduced by these technologies are beyond accountability. The hazards of these technologies are potentially catastrophic to the degree that the collapse of industrial civilization is a logically foreseeable outcome. When we add EROEI energy analysis to the risk scenarios of our complex society, the extreme dilemma of the growth economy is not hard to see.

Five Reversals

For those of us living through the flush times from the late 1940s through the 1990s, the reversal of unlimited economic growth is almost unthinkable. But the unthinkable has become the unavoidable. As Kenneth Boulding said in 1965, "In the imagination of those who are sensitive to the realities of our era, Earth has become a spaceship."[35] The big question is, can we safeguard a reasonable and equitable measure of prosperity through the economic re-adaptation that the continued safe functioning of our "spaceship" requires?

In order to get a handle on what is happening to our economy and society, and to consider what a reasonable and effective response might be, it is helpful to consider a series of reversals with which we are now confronted.

1) Fossil fuel use must be drastically reduced and most remaining sources left in the ground.[36] The fossil fuel industries, of course, reject this out of hand, but their recent advertising campaigns indicate that they realize the evidence is building toward this conclusion. The choice is between the scientifically based precautionary principle applied to the long-term common good of the whole commonwealth of life, and the short-term wealth accumulation for a select few of the human species.

2) We can no longer expect that each successive generation will have a more affluent standard of living than the previous one. This reversal is a shock, a wake-up call. It unhinges public faith in the industrial-consumer economy. It hits young people like a betrayal. If the economy can no longer deliver a steadily improving standard of living, then what is the economy for? If it cannot even provide access to the means of life for an increasing number of citizens, then what kind of economy do we have? The evidence of a broken and failing economic system is mounting. Conventional economic thinking has not been able to offer a believable formula for repair or reconstructing a better economic future.

3) The conventional economic model is now suffering a reversal of credibility. The standard economic model is a circular flow involving goods, services, labor, and money. Despite booms and busts, this circular flow of goods and services, labor and wages, investments and contracts, interest and dividends, income and taxes, expenditures and savings, has long been accepted as accurately representing the self-perpetuating activity of economic life in human communities. The fundamental flaw in this model has now become obvious at the intersection of economics and ecology. It fails to account for the stocks of ecosystem capital that feed the economy and the costs of the pollution that the economy creates. It fails to account for the cumulative trajectory of depletion, degradation, and toxification that is steadily reducing Earth's capacity to support life.

4) The monetary and financial system is systematically moving wealth from borrower to lender, from middle and working class folks to corporate elites, and from the poor to the wealthy.[37] The for-profit debt-money system requires governments to increasingly impoverish public services, and load debt on tax payers in order to preserve the privileged status of high-end financial corporations and their wealthy executives and owners. With deregulation and financial innovations, the monetary system is now clearly revealed as a tool of wealth accumulation for the already wealthy.[38]

5) When citizens reduce consumption, increase savings, and refuse debt, they exacerbate economic down turns. When businesses and households are squeezed, they take precautionary action. This new frugality is likely to continue and even increase as businesses and households find new security in reduced expenditure, debt elimination, and increased savings. This reversal is a clear signal that the financial management of the debt-based consumer economy is not working for many people. But this reversal of consumer behavior also stalls economic growth. Less debt is good for households and businesses but bad for the economy. More debt is good for the growth economy but bad for households and businesses.[39]

What Can be Done?

The conventional formula for recovering prosperity is to ramp up the growth of the consumer economy, but we know that our consumer economy is already overshooting the bio-productive and bio-assimilative limits of Earth's ecosystems, and that further growth will accelerate the destruction of Earth's life-support capacity. We generally acknowledge that reducing debt and cutting back on consumption is a good thing, but if consumption is reduced and debts are paid off, the economy stalls. Re-floating the debt-based monetary system is a conventional response, but this will keep the boom-and-bust cycle churning out financial and social insecurity and even calamity. Meanwhile, the structural violence of poverty grinds on, while vast amounts of both cash and capital wealth continue to accumulate in a small number of hands.

Basic economic growth is needed to end poverty in many geographic and cultural zones, but unless zones of wealth and affluence affect a compassionate retreat in material and energy consumption, the growth needed to end poverty will add to the ecological overshoot already bending Earth's ecosystems toward collapse. This consideration of eco-justice stands at the intersection of economics and ecology. Unlike Charles Dickens, who could say in *The Tale of Two Cities,* "It was the best of times, and the worst of times," it looks like the best of times for economic expansion are over, and a big adjustment in economic adaptation is beginning.

The Road Ahead Through
Slightly Tinted Rose-Colored Glasses

The upside of this downward trending impasse, however, is the opportunity to redefine the economy's purpose. A good economy should provide equitable access to the means of life for all people, and preserve and enhance the resources on which human settlement and cultural life depend. A prosperity of "enough" may be possible through a rebirth of social collaboration and ecologically sustainable economic production.[40] Returning to the five reversals outlined above, we can begin to develop a way through and beyond the subsidence of the growth economy.

1) *The prospect of leaving large oil and coal formations in the ground* is, perhaps, the most difficult thought that many of us can imagine. It is not likely that renewable energy technology can be scaled up in time within the capitalist market system to compensate for a dramatic reduction in the use of fossil fuels. This means that capitalism is not up to the task of facilitating the transition to renewable energy within a safe timeframe. But does renewable energy technology need to match the output of current fossil fuel technology? Perhaps a quite reasonable way of life can be organized and enjoyed around a much lower use of energy.

We already have the renewable energy technology we need; it can be widely and flexibly deployed, and the economic activity around its manufacture, installation, and maintenance will provide a significant level of jobs and income.[41] For the full benefit of renewable energy to be rolled out in a way that supports a reasonable prosperity, it will probably have to be done in a public trust economic framework, very much like that which was widely accepted during the Second World War. This means politics must get serious about whether or not we want to live in a society that pulls together for the common good. Public policy and legislation will be determined by how this question is answered.

2) *The living standard prospects of the current and coming generations* can be addressed in a subsiding economy by recognizing that the previously secure link between jobs and income has been broken for many people and households, and is unlikely to be restored. As discussed in detail in Chapter Five, access to the means of life can be placed within an income support and employment framework. Through a platform of basic income, stakeholder grants, and public

31

interest employment, re-attachment to an economy of measured prosperity could be established. Although the material standard of living may change, a subsiding economy need not be impoverishing if the activities, vocations, employment, and jobs that make for a satisfying, secure, and dignified way of life are supported by a non-profit, public trust monetary system. This scenario depends on a package of policies and legislation that emerges from a genuine public interest political process.

3) The circular flow model of the economy may still be taught in economics classes, but natural capital is now an acknowledged and important part of economic analysis. Procedures are being developed to construct an accurate and full cost accounting for the use of material and energy sources, especially in Europe. But North American leaders in business and government are still a long way from talking realistically about a sustainable economy. For example, imported fruits and vegetables should be steadily increasing in cost as the result of carbon pricing on fossil fuels, thus providing a competitive incentive for local production.

Import replacement is the key to building a resilient economy.[42] For example, urban agriculture is now a bright spot that can ensure a continued measure of prosperity, as the global supply lines of industrialized food production fall victim to the EROEI descent. The EROEI descent will also open up a renaissance of opportunity for local and regional manufacturing, processing, and repair businesses.[43] If this redevelopment of local and regional economies proceeds on the basis of resource stock maintenance, energy conservation, and materials recycling, the subsidence of the industrial-commercial era could balance out into a steady-state conserver economy of fair prosperity. Public policies and smart legislation should support the revitalization of local food systems and the redevelopment of local manufacturing and repair businesses.

4) A collective reconsideration of the purpose of the monetary system arises from the question of the purpose of the economy. If general agreement can be reached that a good economy should provide equitable access to the means of life for all people, and preserve and enhance the resources on which human settlement and cultural life depend, then the way the monetary system works becomes a matter of critical importance.[44]

Most modern governments have placed the operation and control of their national currency system in the hands of for-profit financial corporations. But why should a sovereign government, which has the essential authority to create and regulate the national currency, default on this responsibility in favor of the private banking industry? Why should a national government have to borrow the national currency from private banks? Why should a government have to pay millions in interest on borrowed money? None of this is necessary; it is simply an historically determined convention. The monetary system could just as well be set up as a non-profit, public service institution that insures adequate circulation of legal tender to all citizens, and fund public interest expenditures on a debt-free basis.[45]

5) Reducing consumption, getting out of debt, and increasing the means of local provisioning will increase security as the economy subsides to a level well within Earth's bio-capacity limits. Our sense of prosperity, security, and dignity will flow from solid social attachment, vibrant community commerce, and a rich flourishing of local and regional culture. If a national, non-profit, public service monetary system can be put in place, and a range of resilient local currencies emerge in many communities, we will have a platform on which a variety of other precautionary and conserver policies and practices can be developed, implemented, and supported. A subsiding economy may then be able to settle around an ecologically sound steady state, in which a reasonable and equitable level of prosperity can be maintained.[43] All of this will take a rebirth of broad support for public interest politics and governance for the common good.

Good Growth, De-Growth, or Steady-State No-Growth?

Three linked factors condition the prospects of our economy whether we are thinking in terms of good growth, de-growth, or steady-state no-growth.

1) The falling ratio of energy return on energy investment (EROEI) for oil extraction will eventually end the market economy's ability to provide this form of energy;

2) There is insufficient thermal capacity in the atmosphere to safely accommodate the combustion of all known oil and gas deposits; and

3) There are not enough earnings in the world to amortize presently accumulated debt.

The hope that continued economic growth can solve the debt dilemma runs head-on into the atmosphere's thermal capacity and the falling EROEI ratio. As our economy attempts to cope with them, the relationships between these three factors will have a direct bearing on employment and living standards, energy availability, the way the economy works, the design and functioning of the monetary system, and the emergence of a post-consumer, measured and sustainable prosperity.

Although our discussions of good growth, de-growth, and steady-state no-growth sound like we are talking about opposing concepts and expectations, in reality, all of these movements will likely be in play as we proceed into an uncertain future. Even as certain kinds of unsustainable economic activity stop growing and decline, other kinds of sustainable activity will emerge and grow. Two prime examples are oil-dependent food systems on the de-growth side, and food systems that are based on enriching organic soil fertility and various forms of renewable energy on the growth side. Likewise, in transportation we will probably see a decline in personal fossil fuel vehicles and growth in the use of public transport.

Another example appears in the fate of global trade and the potential for resurgence of local manufacturing. Global trade is intimately connected to oil pricing. Jeff Rubin calculates that when petroleum hits $150 to $200 a barrel it will no longer be profitable to run container ships from Asia to North America.[46] All the industries and businesses connected to this trade will collapse, but the growth of local manufacturing will then have the opportunity to flourish. Eventually, after a protracted period of decline in some sectors and the growth of sustainable practices in others, a dynamically balanced steady-state economy, within the boundaries of ecosystem capacities, may come to be a new operating system for human habitation on spaceship Earth.

CHAPTER FIVE
Meaningful Jobs and Livelihoods
Stephen Loughin

Introduction

There is a growing sense that the global recession of 2008-2012 is not an ordinary down-turn in the business cycle, nor is it simply the collapse of yet another economic bubble—this time in housing. Instead, something fundamental has shifted, as if economic foundations thought to be set upon bedrock are instead resting on quicksand. While politicians argue about how to rekindle economic growth, it appears that we may have already reached the natural growth limit of a debt-based economy. These economic and ecological limits call into question how we will find jobs or make a living if full employment depends so directly on growth. In this essay, we consider how we might adapt to an economy that is contracting toward a sustainable steady-state, but still find purposeful work to make a life that is spiritually fulfilling and meaningful.

What is Work?

In Neolithic times, humans lived in small groups that subsisted by hunting and gathering. The essentials of life were water, food, shelter and clothing. Life was defined by the daily and seasonal occupations needed to go on living. Every individual was required to gather and hunt for food, tend the herds of livestock, or cultivate the soil. Preparing and preserving food, making clothing, baskets, pottery, weapons, simple tools, and constructing shelters rounded out the activities of daily life. The economic model for these people relied on communal effort and communal sharing. The economic output of each person's work was directly rewarded by sufficient water, food, and shelter, to be shared among the members of the community.[47]

While few would want this lifestyle today, it is interesting to note that the amount of time spent hunting or gathering food was often substantially less than most of us work today, at least those of us fortunate enough to have a job. Work sustained those hunters and gatherers, and when that sustenance was sufficient, it gave way to leisure. Today, the hunting and gathering done in the workplace is almost always metaphorical: hunting for new sales prospects, foraging for data and information. For most of us, work has become entirely disconnected from food and the other essentials of life. Another feature is that work is generally organized by others. Except for the 11 percent who are self-employed, to work is to be employed by another. The word "employ" literally means "to shape to one's use." Even those who are self-employed generally do their work for others.

Evolution of Livelihoods

The development of irrigation agriculture 5,000 years ago in Egypt, India, and Mesopotamia allowed farmers to produce a surplus. This extra food enabled a few of the people to be released from the daily task of food production, and to specialize in other arts and crafts.[46] This birth of the leisure class coincided with the birth of cities of several thousand or even tens of thousands, which were organized by a collaboration between politics and religion.[48] The majority of individuals still had to work at food production, but the surplus was collected as a tribute to a king or a deity, and stored in the king's granary or in the temple. Enforcement of payment created a new class of specialists doing work that did not directly result in production of water, food, clothing or shelter.

In these early societies, the stored grain formed the basic economic unit of value. Moving grain around to facilitate trade was inconvenient, so tokens became accepted and people became accustomed to working in exchange for money with the assumption that the money could be used to buy food, shelter, and clothing. The managerial class, the kings, nobility, and high priests, came to regard themselves as owners of the means of production: the herds, fields, rivers, and the working class people. What had previously been held as commonwealth, was now considered private property. The economic model had fundamentally shifted from communal to feudal.

Employment Today

Fast forward 5,000 years or so, and people now live in cities of hundreds of thousands or millions of individuals. It is hard to call these communities, though certainly communities exist within these metropolises. The chart on page 37 shows the distribution of employment in the U.S. in the 2012 census.[49] Because of the industrialization of

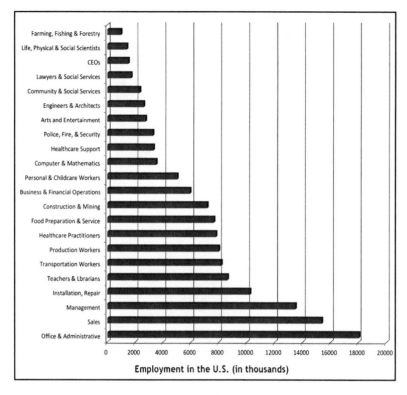

Employment in the U.S. (in thousands)

agriculture, fewer than one percent in the U.S. work directly in farming, fishing, or raising animals for food. Fully a third of people work in management, administrative, office, and sales jobs. CEOs form just over one percent of the workforce. Once a much larger segment of the workforce, only about 10 percent are involved in manufacturing production, construction and mining today. Instead, a larger number are involved in food preparation and food service. But those statistics are for the 139 million who are fortunate enough to have work.

Unemployment in the U.S.

Unemployment statistics from 1890 to 2010 are shown in the graph on page 38.[50] A disproportionate number of these unemployed are young people, especially young men of color. The Bureau of Labor Statistics (BLS) reports that among young people, aged 16-24, the total unemployment rate between April and July of 2011 ranged from 17 to 19 percent. Among African-American youth in this age group, the rate was 28 to 31 percent. Among Hispanic and Latino youth, it was 18 to 21 percent.[51] In addition, the BLS data does not include the long-term

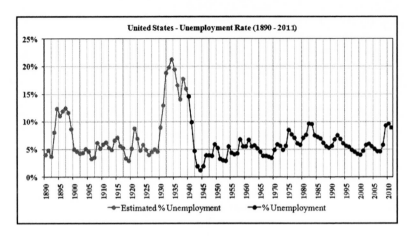

United States - Unemployment Rate (1890 - 2011)

—♦— Estimated % Unemployment   —●— % Unemployment

unemployed, those who have stopped looking for jobs or have taken part-time work because they cannot find full time employment in their field. An alternative metric that includes these people, suggests that at the peak of the recent recession, the actual 2010 unemployment/underemployment was about 22 percent.[52]

Why are so many unemployed or underemployed?

In the U. S., the recession began in December 2007 and was officially declared over in June of 2009. However, if one uses the job market as the barometer of recession, it is still ongoing in 2012. Politicians on the right and left are deadlocked, but both argue that it is essential to restart growth in order to solve the employment problem. Unfortunately, it appears that we have reached the point that global growth is unsustainable.

Another major factor causing unemployment is globalization. The maximum profit for global enterprise is to manufacture products in a place where raw material and labor costs are almost nothing and sell those products in a market where they command the highest prices. This creates problems at both ends of the supply chain. In the places where they are manufacturing products, they are often engaged in unethical or corrupt practices to avoid the full cost of environmental damage and fair labor practices. In the places where they sell their products, they are no longer employing people except in administration and sales. Each company hopes that somebody else will provide the good jobs that will enable people to afford their products. To some extent, this worked during the housing bubble leading up to the 2008 recession, with people borrowing against the equity in their homes to sustain their consumer lifestyle. Since 2008 this trend has reversed and savings rates

38

have gone up. Many companies are finding demand for their products insufficient to justify adding employees, and so we remain mired in economic doldrums.

A third factor undermining employment is the robot. Factories are becoming more and more automated, and even many customer service functions are handled by speech-recognizing computer programs. It may soon be possible to manufacture products with almost no human labor at all. Though robots are expensive, they work around the clock, never ask for a raise, and don't care if the lights are on.

Finally, from a macroeconomic perspective, one might say that our unemployment problem is really due to a lack of money. Since our money is debt based, this means a lack of credit. Smaller companies and individuals cannot borrow money now that banks are more risk averse. Larger companies are hoarding cash and do not need to borrow. All of this means that less money is being created in the form of loans, and therefore there is less money to purchase the goods and services that could lead to more employment. While people on the right, such as Ron Paul, and on the left, such as Dennis Kucinich, have both proposed moving away from a debt-based monetary system, the political middle remains deadlocked and unable to consider any meaningful policy changes.

The age of a secure job with a corporate employer is over. Industry has fled to cheaper labor markets. Retailers have mega-sized their footprint and minimized their labor needs, stocking products made in faraway places. Local government and education jobs are disappearing as tax revenues shrink. So much of our identity has been bound up with what we do for a living that it is difficult to grapple with the question of what we can do when that living goes away. It is time to decide, once again, what we want to be when we grow up.

What Do I Want To Be When I Grow Up?

To answer this question requires that we be bold, and embark with a new vision that takes us past these traditional modes of employment and sidesteps these conventional employers. A sustainable economy is emerging, one that we hope will not have to wait, like a phoenix, to rise from the ashes of a burned-out growth economy before it can flourish. As Quakers, we are called to live in the "now and not yet" kingdom of God, and likewise we must become adept at living in a world where both the old and the new economies exist side-by-side. Our success at this will depend upon becoming generalists, like our grandparents and great-grandparents before us. It may be that we build our livelihood in pieces, with some things done for cash money and others done in trade, or in exchange with others for labor hours. All of this will depend upon reawakening our sense of community and understanding the interdependence we have, not only with one another, but with all the parts of God's creation.

Rethinking the Professions

The professions have changed dramatically as our economy evolved from a local, agricultural orientation to an industrial orientation, to a post-industrial-service economy that is global in scope but devoid of responsibility. Once upon a time, the steady professions were butcher, baker, and candlestick-maker, if one believes the nursery rhyme. Note the prominence of food-professions there. Then there were doctors, lawyers, and native-American chiefs. In other words: healthcare, law, and management. In the information age, the computer and engineering professions joined these ranks. Today most professionals are engaged in the employ of larger enterprises. Doctors work for hospitals and healthcare corporations, lawyers work for government, corporations or big law firms, and managers work for all of the above and corporations as well. Fewer and fewer of us are set up in individual practice. Mostly, this banding together is to limit liability, and one might assert that the need for this formal accountability is, at least in part, due to the lack of any real relationship to a community.

Rebuilding community will be essential to a sustainable future. The economy of this community will be focused on local agriculture, local commerce, local government, and local professionals. Some professions are difficult to outsource offshore. Plumbing, carpentry, mechanical repair, and maintenance work are examples of work that has to be done locally. Likewise, the healthcare professions are mostly person-to-person, though some experiments in remote care have been tried. The likely prospect of having the "new" and "old" economies co-existing for a time will create a need for professionals willing to bridge this divide.

The new economy will require more people to work in the reuse, repair, recycle tripod that supports sustainability. Clearly, we can no longer buy and throw away as much as we do now, as there is no longer any "away." Once milk was delivered in reusable glass bottles and this will be the norm again. Cradle-to-cradle design is essential, and this new engineering approach will open up opportunities for both professionals and labor.[53]

In 2011, top medical specialists earned about $156 per hour in the U.S., almost 10 times as much as the median hourly wage of $16.[54] Many of the "new" economic models rely on even, hour-for-hour exchange which may not appeal to professionals used to such high compensation. However, the hourly rate for many professionals has been dropping as new people enter these fields and as healthcare corporations find new ways to convert overall healthcare expenditures into profits. Hopefully, this will convince some professionals to participate in both the new and old economies. Indeed many doctors and lawyers already donate some of their time in clinics and other pro-bono work in their communities.

Apprenticeships and Reskilling for Work

Apprenticeships were once common practice, but have fallen from favor as the developed west has moved away from actually making things and toward simply consuming things. However, they have remained popular in some of the more successful economies around the world, including Germany, Austria, France, Canada, and Australia. While there is a dark side to the practice in which the apprenticeship is used to keep a craft closed to all but a select few, there is much to be said for the transfer of skill and art from an experienced practitioner to a younger generation. Germany has successfully used a dual track model for education in which children are tested and those with certain aptitudes are steered toward apprenticeships rather than university.

Economic viability in a sustainable economy, especially during the painful transition from growth to no-growth, belongs to the generalist. The person who has a broad foundation of skills will be able to cobble together a living from pieces. The recent Transition Town (TT) movement has recognized the importance of revitalizing our skills inventory, and recommends that we undertake a conscious effort to share our skills and knowledge within our communities. Who among us remembers how to can fruits and vegetables, weave cloth, build furniture, or repair bicycles? Developing skill-sharing networks can be fun and rewarding. Meetings and individual Friends are becoming involved in TT projects like the Friendly Households that seek to share skills within the community.

Open Source Education

One of the hardest hit areas of the economy, as state and local tax base shrinks, has been education. Unfortunately, this is very much like eating one's seed corn during a famine. Short-changing our children's education will reduce their prospects for high-paying jobs that could support a higher tax base in the future, and will increase their chance of needing social service intervention or becoming involved in crime. One model for addressing the critical need for education in the face of a serious decline in the capacity of our traditional education infrastructure is the "open-source" model.

Wikipedia is an example of how an open-source approach to a knowledge-base can eventually eclipse the traditional encyclopedia. While it is criticized by traditional scholars for the occasional disinformation or blatantly incorrect article, this community approach to building and maintaining informative articles has resulted in an enormous cache of useful information. Any person who finds an error is free to edit the article and correct the problems that they see. Over time, articles tend to become fairly authoritative, often drawing input from world leaders in specific disciplines. The model includes methods for dealing with contentious topics in which differing opinions are presented; so a balanced sampling of the points of view are presented.

Recently, major universities have started putting course-ware online as an open source experiment. Lectures are available as audio or video streams. Anyone can sign up for these courses at no cost, and there is even homework which is graded by other students or volunteers who are advanced students in these fields. Some of these open-source courses now have subscriptions in the tens of thousands. It remains to be seen how credentials will be handled with this approach. But perhaps the diploma is only a convenience for large, bureaucratic employers, a substitute for really getting to know potential employees. If a person has a degree from a university in electrical engineering, then we assume s/he can design an electrical circuit. Yet there are many who have the degree but lack the ability, and likewise many with the ability who lack the degree.

Services or Products?

The sustainable economy of the future will likely comprise more services and fewer products that consume resources, especially if the resources cannot be recaptured for future re-use. It will be important to make our limited purchases of resources and energy go as far as possible. This will push the focus toward products that are more central to our survival and well-being. Current designs are intended to last only a few months or years before being replaced, but products we buy in the future will have to be sustainably manufactured and reliable, reparable, and recyclable. Thoughtful purchasers will consider whether the laborers involved in making the product were fairly compensated for their work. We will no longer throw away even small amounts of irreplaceable metals found in small electronic devices. The good news is that this shift in priorities will open up new service-sector jobs in sustainable design, repair, and recycling.

Shortening the Work Week

One obvious solution to unemployment and underemployment is to shorten the work week. If there is 10 percent unemployment, then cutting the work week from 40 hours to 36 hours should mean that in order to accomplish the same amount of work, about 10 percent more people would need to be hired. Since there is actually more like 20 percent unemployment, then the work week should be about 32 hours.

Employees would give up 10-20 percent of their compensation and employers would have to increase their benefit expenses to put more people on the payroll. The shift could be done over a period of years, and tax policy could be used to encourage compliance. For example, the employer portion of payroll taxes on overtime pay could be increased to eliminate the perceived advantage of making fewer workers do more work. The allowances made for professional employees who have traditionally been salaried (meaning they are paid a fixed amount regardless of how many hours they work) could be restricted to those who have a significant ownership stake in the business. This could encourage a shift to cooperative employers and other employee-owned businesses.

Job Sharing

For many people, the 40-hour work week does not balance with childcare, eldercare, and other responsibilities. Flexible job-sharing would enable people to work just the mornings or just the afternoons, or perhaps work fewer days each week. While employers are often reluctant to enter into job-sharing arrangements, there are significant benefits of having two people working some tasks. A person who is doing something for only four hours is much less likely to experience burnout than one who is at the job eight hours a day. When jobs involve problem solving, often two heads are better than one. In care-giving jobs, the sharing can involve a brief period of overlap in which information about patients can be exchanged. Some of this is already happening informally as employers use part-time workers without benefits to fill full-time jobs. Formalizing job sharing and deciding how best to handle benefits can make this transition work better for both employees and employers. A change in tax policy to encourage employers to provide essential benefits to part-time employees would aid the success of this approach.

Most of those who participate in the community-based, ecologically integrated economy of the future will need to keep a toe in the money-based, growth economy because many critical items needed for daily life will be slow to move away from the old economy, and job-sharing provides a way to do that.

Rethinking the Work = Money Equation

Key to this discernment is the need to understand the role of money in our lives. We have been taught to believe that if we do not earn much money for our work, we will not prosper. However, money is really just one way of facilitating the economic exchanges or trades that enable us to live. We need to do something, make something, or provide something that others find valuable, and then find a way of exchanging that for the things that we need. If we are clever, money need not always be involved. Moreover, finding ways of exchanging value without money will rebuild the fabric of our communities that have been so damaged by our present economic model.

People have been accepting money in payment for work for thousands of years. To walk away from a job that pays "real money" in favor of other arrangements would seem ludicrous to most people. And yet, we already know that the money is not real in any sense other than the goods and services that we exchange for it. Direct bartering is usually too cumbersome to be practical on a large scale, but several other schemes have been proposed as methods of paying for work.

One is the time bank, in which work is traded on an hour-for-hour basis. One might trade an hour of plumbing in exchange for an hour of electrical wiring, for example. Any needed parts and materials are either compensated as expenses or directly provided by the person receiving the services. Using the web, there are a few systems that support community time banks so that you do not have to only exchange work with people who can do things you need to have done. These systems keep an account of how many hours each person has given, and how many hours each person has received. That way, it does not matter if hours are given to one person, but received from a different person, as long as it balances out within the overall community. People can donate hours so time banks can also be used to organize community support services for members who can no longer provide hours.[55]

Another way of facilitating trade without official money is the use of an alternative currency. This has happened many times in the past, often employing some generally useful item or staple. Roman soldiers were sometimes paid in salt, while frontier trappers and traders used hides or pelts like the buck-skin. More recently, in an effort to aid their local economies, towns have printed their own alternative currencies. Usually, these have an established exchange rate with the official currency. Local merchants agree to accept them for goods and services. Ithaca, New York, was one of the early adopters of a local currency they called "Ithaca Hours,"[56] and in western Massachusetts, over 2. 5 million BerkShares have circulated.[57]

The likely solution for most communities will be to have a mix of such strategies available. These alternatives to money create problems for taxing authorities. Because in the old economy, the value of an hour of plumbing was not the same as an hour of babysitting, these types of exchanges are considered uneconomic exchanges and are not usually taxed. That may change if alternatives become more common. Some alternative currencies that have an official exchange rate for ordinary money are taxed as if the transaction used official currency. However, most taxing authorities decline to accept the alternative currency. For local governments there may be significant advantages in allowing citizens to pay their taxes in alternative currency, time bank hours, or both. Municipal and township employees may be quite willing to accept part of their pay in alternative currencies if there is wide acceptance by local merchants. Ultimately, the strength and resilience of the community will depend upon the ability to bring together both local labor and local resources to accomplish cooperative community projects that would have been paid for by a new municipal bond issue in the old economy. We can no longer afford to go deeper in debt as communities.

Basic Income and Safety Nets

The idea of a basic income, paid as a grant by the government traces to Thomas Paine, who suggested in 1795 that estate and land taxes be used to provide an old-age pension and also a grant of a fixed sum to citizens upon reaching the age of majority as just compensation for the loss of "inheritance" of the commons that have been converted to private ownership.[58]

The question of whether society could afford the provision of a basic income was largely resolved in the 1960s when the cost of providing a minimally adequate basic income was shown to be less than the costs of the safety net and welfare programs it would replace. This continues to be the case.[59]

If a basic income were provided, those who are unable to find work would at least be able to survive. A basic income might free people to engage in work that is meaningful and fulfilling, but not valued economically, like arts and crafts, which would free people to pursue their own dreams. A basic minimum income would be a foundation from which most people would naturally seek additional income from a job or self-employment enterprise. The few content to live frugally on a basic income could do so.

The provision of a basic income would likely trigger a sharp drop in crimes of theft motivated by penury. The negative effects on health associated with poverty, both physical and emotional, would be greatly ameliorated. The falling social costs of crime and ill health would be a boon to society and government budgets. In addition, the psychological effect of knowing that one is part of a society and political economy that values your security and well-being is likely to have a positive impact on one's motivation for social and political engagement. This is known as "the stakeholder effect."[60]

The dark side of a basic income is that it might lead to idleness. At best, this means more couch potatoes watching more hours of TV, and at worst it means more substance abuse and addiction, and perhaps more crimes of aggression and vandalism as those with nothing creative and rewarding to do are often tempted toward ill-considered actions. These could be minimized if communities would provide ample and rewarding opportunities for meaningful social and civic engagement, and a Spirit-led and purpose-filled life is encouraged by the values taught to our youth. The violence and criminal behavior associated with the drug trade must be addressed by political intervention that ends the economic incentive of this underground economy.

Another advantage of a basic income is that it would end the current practice of paying safety net benefits by giving the recipient a pre-loaded debit card backed by one of the major credit card companies. These cards often have an onerous per-use fee that converts a portion of the benefits paid into corporate profits for the card company. Worse, there is a non-use fee of perhaps $5 or $10 per month, which eventually erodes all the benefit value even if the recipient does not use the card. This means that a significant fraction of our spending on social safety nets is actually going to the banks and credit card companies, all for the convenience of providing recipients with plastic money. Integrity demands that non-use fees be outlawed and that the card value revert to the government after a reasonable number of years indicated by a printed expiration date. It should not be going to the banks. Reasonable transaction fees might be justified but certainly not fees for inactivity.

Conclusion

There is a crisis in employment in the United States and most of the developed economies, caused by a convergence of globalization, automation, and looming limits on the growth economy model. An ecologically integrated economy that is built upon a rightly ordered relationship with all of God's creation must emerge. In order to bring this about, we as Friends are called to live in the "now and not yet" world, where two economic models can coexist for a time. The sooner we move to the ecologically integrated model, the less damage we do to our planet and ultimately ourselves.

In order to realize this ecologically integrated economy, we must rethink ideas about how we work and how we contribute to our community. Alternatives exist which enable us to define new, meaningful jobs and livelihoods that truly support and are supported by our community and sustain the community of life around us. None of us will get rich in this alternate economy, but we may lead lives that are blessed by abundant sufficiency and the simple prosperity of a life in right relationship with our world.

CHAPTER SIX
Establishing and Enhancing Responsible Production
Pamela Haines

What is the Role of Production?

This is not a question we generally ask. Production is just part of the economy, which is just part of the way things are. But if we are trying to envision an economy that works in a new way, it is good to start with the big questions. The word economy comes from Greek roots oikos (house) and nemein (to manage), so it can be said that the first economist was the woman who managed a household.[61] Production, then, is for gathering and shaping the resources to pursue individual and social well-being, to maintain our common household. We produce food to eat, clothing to stay warm, housing for shelter, medical infrastructure for health, arts for self-expression and pleasure.

How did our current production system develop?

From time immemorial up until the recent past, most production happened in the home, or in small social groups, and largely for use within those homes or groups. Surplus may have gone to nearby markets or fairs. While there were some long-distance trade routes, greatly expanded in Europe by voyages of exploration starting in the 15th century, most production remained at home. With the Industrial Revolution starting in the 18th century, a whole new world opened up. The use of coal and then oil to power machinery meant that production could be ramped up to a new level. As the end goal of production shifted from use to sale, the role of markets became more central to the process.

This was the context in which our market economy, and production as we know it, blossomed: a lightly populated planet, powerful new energy sources, and seemingly unlimited supplies of natural resources. The drive to do things faster and better was compelling. Find a way to weave more cloth, harvest more wheat, move more goods, store food longer, mine coal deeper. Anybody with the ability to gather labor,

48

energy and natural resources together to produce in a way that added value at the market was well situated to prosper and grow.

This model of economic growth and production has space for an ever-increasing population, assumes an abundant supply of energy and resources, and requires an ever-expanding market for what is produced. Many of us still think of our economy this way, associating it with the open range and limitless horizons. Yet in the last half-century or so we have been witnessing a variety of developments that call those basic assumptions and requirements into question.

What has changed?

Our once lightly populated planet has become crowded, uncomfortably so in many places. We are running through the easily accessible fossil fuels (stored sunlight from hundreds of millions of years ago) that made our industrial revolution possible. As mining of other finite resources continues unabated, extraction costs are beginning to rise. The assumption that unwanted by-products of production (heat, air and water pollutants, mine tailings, processing chemicals) could just be emitted, abandoned, or thrown away is being challenged by the growing awareness that ultimately there is no "away" where they can be thrown without consequence. A production process that seemed to work fine in centuries past is just not a good fit for our current spaceship Earth.

Furthermore, the system's demand for ever-increasing markets for an ever-increasing supply of goods is creating distortions in patterns of consumption. The market for many products in this country is saturated. Thus producers shift from meeting real needs to using advertising to create and distort "wants," filling the airwaves with an incessant message that our happiness depends on purchasing the next new thing and filling up more shelf space in stores with an ever-increasing array of choices for the same basic item—toothpaste, shampoo, or tomato sauce. This is an enormous affront to our basic Quaker principles of simplicity and integrity. Many products which could last for years are produced with a profit-seeking eye toward rapid obsolescence, either through using cheap materials that quickly wear out or parts that cannot be replaced, creating an urgent need for the latest style in clothing or athletic shoes, or the latest generation of electronic devices.

While some people in our country still lack things that would increase their well-being in a tangible way and many more around the world are in desperate need of basics; our production system is not geared toward meeting such basic needs, nor do those in need have access to the resources to make such purchases. It is ironic that a system which prides itself on minimizing costs through labor saving technology is putting people out of work who are needed to buy its products.

The Structure of our Production System

We find ourselves at a fork in the road. More of the same will lead us to a dead end, as we heedlessly run through ever-scarcer resources and put precious fossil fuel energy into creating things that we do not need. It can even be plausibly argued that the goals of our economic-financial system are no longer focused on production at all. Sound and viable businesses are being swallowed by multinationals that can do buy-outs with more profit and less effort than actually producing anything of value themselves. Private equity firms can make a killing from buying up companies, gutting and bleeding them, laying off workers or fleecing them of their retirement benefits and walking away with the assets, just to repeat the process all over again. A poignant commentary on this sorry state of affairs comes from a maker of Odwalla juices: "When our corporation was privately owned, we were in the business of making a product; once we went public, we were in the business of making money."[62]

The majority of American citizens, who used to play a role in producing the goods we all need, have been consigned to the role of consumers. Production happens somewhere else. We have been told that our most important contribution to the economy—our patriotic duty—is to shop. Clearly our production system has strayed off course. We need to find our way back to the basic values that underlie the model of the common household working together to produce what is needed for the welfare of its members.

History of the corporation

What would the other fork in the road look like? It will help to start with a review of the history of the corporation, the heart of our current system of production. The British East India Company was an early model, chartered by the monarchy in 1600 with a fifteen-year monopoly on trade with East India and Africa. It was able to both raise huge amounts from shareholders to engage in this trade, and return huge profits. As the British colonies in North America formed into a new country, the right to charter corporations was kept with the states.

The standard practice was to charter a corporation for a particular purpose, and for a particular length of time. The corporation got the advantage of raising money to do its business from many stockholders; the state, in turn, got a say in what corporations were chartered to do and raised revenue through its right of taxation.

The balance between public and private rights and interests began to change in the late 1800's with Supreme Court language endorsing a view that the 14th Amendment conferred on corporations the same legal status and protections it created for human beings, The role of states in shaping the purpose and life-span of corporate charters gradually eroded, and when Delaware passed an act in 1899 to attract businesses through low corporate registration fees and taxation, corporations flocked there, further insulating them from local control. Thus a structure that was the creation of the state, chartered to help do its business and serve at its pleasure, has broken free from those constraints. Our dominant form of business enterprise has become essentially immortal, while claiming the rights of personhood.[63]

Corporate Governance

The classical understanding of corporate governance is that the managers of a corporation, as employees of its owners, have a moral duty to carry out the wishes of those shareholders who, in the main, invest in order to make a profit, and that maximal profits coincide with maximal contribution to social well-being.[64] Thus, even well-intentioned and community-minded corporate leaders are disallowed from pursuing social goals that might negatively impact the bottom line. This is the context in which it is better to buy out other companies than expand one's own production, to resist regulation, to relocate to areas where labor is cheaper and taxes are lower, and to buy political favor.

The buying of political favor took an enormous step forward with the U.S. Supreme Court's 2010 Citizens United ruling, reaffirming that corporations have the rights of personhood and that corporate contributions to political campaigns are a form of free speech. Yet this step toward greater corporate control of our electoral process should come as no surprise. For decades enormous and powerful multinational corporations have been flexing their muscles, wringing concessions from governments, expanding their ability to roam the globe freely, seeking the lowest labor costs and most lax environmental standards, heedless of the impact on local communities, intent solely on pursuing profit.

51

This form of enterprise now threatens not only our ability to apply ethical considerations to our system of production but our very democracy.

The Citizens United ruling, along with the Occupy movement, has brought wider attention to the problematic nature of our corporate-dominated system of production. A scattering of local governments have been challenging the right of corporations for years, passing ordinances that forbid certain kinds of operations within their boundaries; those precedents are being studied and copied more widely. A vigorous grassroots movement has sprung up to work for a constitutional amendment to clarify once and for all that corporations are not people.

Cooperatives

Any attempt to change these systems must include both a challenge to the power structures that hold them in place, and the creation of alternatives that can grow to take over the role they play. Luckily, alternatives abound. Cooperatives are a vital part of our current production system. According to a recent University of Wisconsin study, while most of the 30,000 cooperatives in the United States are consumer coops, seven million Americans are members of producer and purchasing coops, 42 million are served by electric utility coops, and three million are members of agricultural coops. Overall, the cooperative sector owns $3 trillion in assets, generates a half-trillion dollars a year in revenue, and pays 856,000 people $25 billion in annual wages.[65]

Clearly this sector, more closely attuned to the general welfare of people and communities and less tightly tied to a single bottom line, is one whose expansion would benefit a whole Earth economy. Quakers are closely attuned with these underlying principles (equality, community, integrity) and have been active in a variety of ways to promote cooperative production throughout our history.[66]

Triple bottom line

There has also been promising movement in recent years to create corporations whose charters allow for a triple bottom line: not just profit, but people and planet as well. Most commonly known as "for-benefit corporations," they have been accepted as legal entities in several states. A system of certification has been developed, and interest in them as an alternative to traditional corporations has grown rapidly as more and more people rise to the challenge of responsible production.

Small Businesses

Finally there are all the small businesses that are financed without stockholders. These businesses, rooted in their communities, are more amenable to following local ordinances, addressing local needs and responding to local input than multinational corporations, which are often headquartered half a continent away. They recirculate wealth more effectively in local communities. Philosophically, small businesses also fit with the overall concept of subsidiarity—the organizing principle that matters ought to be handled by the smallest, lowest or least centralized competent authority.

Quaker Contributions

Since the beginnings of the Religious Society of Friends in the 17th century, Quakers have been translating their religious convictions into thought and action on issues of the economy and society. John Bellers' concern for the poor in the late 1600s included incisive economic analysis and an innovative proposal that was used 150 years later in the development of the cooperative movement.[67]

In the late 1700s, John Woolman showed an intuitive understanding of "right relationship" with regard to the land, the use and care of animals, and the disruption, degradation, and exploitation of labor that occur under the dominion of privilege and wealth accumulation. In the midst of the Great Depression, some Friends were thinking deeply about how to end that economic and social catastrophe, and others were deeply involved in Roosevelt's New Deal.[68]

In the current-day, Friends in their monthly and yearly meetings, and through organizations such as the American Friends Service Committee (AFSC), Friend Committee on National Legislation, Quaker Earthcare Witness and Quaker Instiute for the Future, have been acting upon their religious convictions in their concerns for integrity in our economic systems. For example, a working group within the AFSC developed a set of principles that would characterize a nonviolent economy, including trusteeship, cooperation, democracy, social development, human orientation, and equal access.[69]

Changing Technologies for a Changing World

The structures and values that dominate our current economic system are ill-suited to get us out of the bind we are in. The existence of other more flexible and responsive structures provides a hopeful indication of ways forward. But it does not get to the heart of the issue of how production can be maintained in a finite planet.

With labor in Western countries as an increasingly expensive part of the production process over the decades, the focus of technological innovation on saving labor has been a straightforward and logical one. Why pay a pricey person if you could get a machine, created from cheap materials by cheap energy, to do the job as well or even better? Once again, it is hard to get our minds around the reality that natural resources and energy, along with the ability of Earth to absorb our wastes, are now the limiting factors. We are facing a future where productive processes that use less resources and energy, and more human labor, will be better positioned to address the dual issues of scarce resources and high unemployment. It is time to completely rethink our concept of efficiency.

Shifting agriculture

Agricultural production provides a striking illustration. In the evolution of industrial agriculture, not only has the goal steadily shifted away from supporting farm families and feeding the community. The shift toward a big-business focus on short-term profit maximization has created a system that is heavily dependent on fossil fuels. Its combined components (petroleum-based fertilizers and pesticides, big farm machinery, processing, packaging and long-distance trucking) consume more energy than the food energy they produce, and would not even be profitable without government farm and fuel subsidies.

Renewable technology

There is growing interest in renewable technology these days, particularly in the area of energy conservation. Renewable and alternative energy systems have finally made it into the mainstream with a wide array of technological developments. Standards have been developed for green buildings that are more energy efficient. We have finally seen some movement in the production of cars that get significantly more miles to the gallon, though the limiting factor there is not the technology, but the political environment in terms of regulatory requirements and financial incentives. Standards have become stricter around greenhouse gas emissions from industry, which has led to technological innovations in some production processes. The interest in alternatives to industrial, chemical-based agriculture is steadily growing.

Technology has been a powerful driver of progress for hundreds of years, and it can continue to create greater energy and resource efficiencies, but we cannot simply put our trust in it to lead us out of the dilemmas we currently face. To the extent that technological solutions require significant inputs of finite fuels and natural resources, they need to be evaluated very carefully. One of the rarely discussed issues in the debate about nuclear power is the energy and environmental cost of mining ever-lower grade supplies of uranium ore. More problematic for energy-conscious consumers is the debate about whether the batteries for some of the new highly fuel-efficient cars use more energy than they save. The energy required to mine the metals, then to transport, store, handle and recycle the hazardous materials must be considered, as well as the environmental damage sustained in the mining.

Living sustainably on Planet Earth

These innovations and changes in a variety of sectors of the economy are an excellent start in addressing the problem of peak oil and the link between greenhouse gas emissions and climate change. But they do not get to the heart of what needs to change in our production systems so that we can live sustainably on Planet Earth.

Debate rages about the extent of the supply of minerals left in the ground and the years they could last, with data organized to bolster or refute deeply held and sharply divergent philosophical positions. Yet resources are finite. There are troubling indications that the metals we know, like copper, and other rare transition metals we hardly know— indium, gallium, palladium, tantalum—but need for cutting-edge technologies, including solar panels, will be in dangerously short supply by the end of this century, if not before.[70] And the argument that new technologies can find more supplies and process ever-lower grade ores still assumes there are no limits on easy access to energy for extraction or the capacity of Earth's systems to absorb pollution. Nor does it question the limitations of the technological process itself.

Renowned Quaker scientist, Ursula Franklin, argues that the spread of technology has become self-reinforcing in a way that can hinder viable and appropriate political or economic change, and cause humans to become servants to technological requirements, rather than actively engaging in creation and decision-making. She questions any technological fix that does not also promote justice; restore reciprocity; confer divisible or indivisible benefits; maximize gain or minimize disaster; and favor people over machines, conservation over waste, and the reversible over the irreversible.[71]

Circular production

We need to dig deeper, and probe assumptions about production that have gone essentially unchallenged for centuries. Since the Enlightenment and the Scientific and Industrial Revolutions, we have tended to think in a linear model: progress, knowledge, mastery of the environment, and humanity in general are all on an upward trajectory; the line moves steadily forward and always up.

It should be no surprise that our traditional production systems conform to that same linear model. Extraction is followed by production, which is followed by consumption, with unused by-products (waste) all along the way. Then there is more extraction, more production, more consumption and more waste. Since both natural resources and the capacity of Earth to absorb waste have seemed unlimited until very recently, this has seemed a straightforward and totally logical approach. Our challenge is to reconceptualize the production process in light of the new realities of our time. As we begin to get our minds around the startling new idea that the economy does not exist in some independent sphere, but is, in fact, embedded in Earth's ecosystems, finite ecosystems, we start to see the necessity of moving toward a model more in line with natural systems and cycles—a model that is more circular than linear.

The idea is to create systems of production where the concept of waste is eliminated altogether. The by-products of any production process, whether in the form of energy or matter, are put to use in a related process. As opposed to the extract-produce-consume-discard system that follows the more traditional "cradle to grave" model, people are calling these "cradle to cradle" technologies. In its purest form, a cradle to cradle system adheres to three basic principles:

1) The waste of one organism or process can become a nutrient for the next;

2) Systems using current solar income do not put the futures of our children and grandchildren at risk; and

3) A technology that mimics nature will celebrate diversity and variety.

The change required in agriculture, for example, has to go beyond tweaking our linear industrial farming methods to be greener and less polluting. The circular process is evident in many organic farming models, where wastes are recycled in such a way that they continually replenish soil fertility. This process can be quite complex, as in the technologies developed at a Fiji boys school around beer waste. The spent grain, mixed with rice straw, becomes a substrate for mushrooms; the mushroom enzymes convert the substrate into more digestible feed for pigs; waste from the pigs is flushed into an anaerobic digester to produce methane, then further digested aerobically in algae ponds; the algae is used as high quality compost for vegetables and for fish food.

What had been just waste is now part of a cycle that produces mushrooms, animal feed, methane, compost and fish food.[72]

In industrial production, the carpet industry has taken initiative, with one company creating a carpet that contains 25% recycled content that can be completely recyclable into new carpet with the company promising to pick up and recycle the old one. In Switzerland, the entire production process of a small fabric mill has been reinvented to produce a toxin-free blend of wool and organically grown ramie, in a process so clean that it generates potable wastewater, and the mill turns scrap trimmings into felt, which Swiss farmers use for mulch in their strawberry fields.[73]

Reparability

Another angle on technology for a spaceship Earth economy is a move from producing with a plan for rapid obsolescence—cars and appliances without repairable parts, software that requires frequent updates, text books, and proprietary batteries—to placing a higher value on durability and the capacity for repair. Just as some companies are now taking responsibility for the disposal of products their customers buy, there are promising initiatives to include a repair commitment in the purchase of a variety of durable goods. With the company assuming responsibility for on-going maintenance, a strong incentive is created to build to last. This could be a step toward a transition in perspective from production of goods to production of services, as in a sale of transport services rather than a sale of cars; so products that are no longer needed are retrieved by the company to be recycled into new ones.

The principles here include closing the loop on materials flow, increasing the intensity and longevity of materials used, and substituting services that are much more eco-friendly for materials. With less employment in production of goods (the need for which is created by planned obsolescence or advertising) there will be more need for employment in maintenance, repair and recycling of our current stock of goods—a welcome reprieve for the stressed stock of natural resources of Planet Earth.

Democracy and Economics
How should production be governed?

Faced with such powerful opposition in the form of giant multinational corporations that make a profit off their dominance of the productive sector in its current form, clearly a transition of this scope will be a challenge. There will need to be both a broad demonstration of public will and government policies that steer us in a new direction, encouraging transition to ownership and technology models that ease the transition to an economy that can endure on a finite planet.

There are at least two major challenges to enacting such government policies: 1) addressing the flaws in the current corporate ownership system, and 2) creating the tax, incentive, and regulatory structures that will encourage truly sustainable production technologies.

For the first challenge, it will be important to take measures to rein in the now virtually unfettered corporations. There are a variety of promising examples of directions forward. Several towns in Maine have passed ordinances forbidding the extraction of their water for sale by for-profit corporations. In late 2010, the Pittsburgh City Council voted unanimously to pass a local ordinance that not only banned natural gas drilling in the city, but recognized rights that have never before been recognized in law, including the right of natural communities and ecosystems.[74]

In the spring of 2011, Bolivia went a big step farther, passing the world's first laws granting all nature equal rights to humans. These rights include:

- the right to life
- the right to exist,
- the right to continue vital cycles and processes free from human alteration,
- the right to pure water and clean air,
- the right to balance,
- the right not to be polluted,
- the right not to have cellular structures modified or genetically altered, and
- the right not to be affected by mega-infrastructure and development projects that affect the balance of ecosystems and the local inhabitant communities.

This Law of Mother Earth redefines the country's rich mineral deposits as "blessings" and is expected to lead to radical new conservation and social measures to reduce pollution and control industry.[75]

Already mentioned have been the moves to amend the Constitution to state clearly that corporations are not people and cannot expect to enjoy the rights of people. Others are working the opposite end, calling for the kind of punishment in response to the law-breaking by corporate "people" that is routinely handed out to regular people. Two public interest groups, for example, have petitioned the Attorney General of Delaware to revoke the charter of Massey Coal, whose disregard for law caused the deaths of 29 miners in 2010, along with incalculable environmental damage, and health risks for residents. They call Massey Coal a criminal enterprise, and note that the corporate charter is a privilege and not a right.[76]

Government can help by establishing systems to review the track record of corporations at regular intervals with the option of revocation. We could learn from the European model where all stakeholders, including workers and community members, sit on corporate boards. Equally important, government can encourage and protect other ownership and production options, such as for-benefit corporations and cooperatives. As of this writing, for-benefit corporation laws have been enacted in seven states and bills are moving forward in seven others.

The second major challenge is to create tax, incentive, and regulatory structures to encourage truly sustainable production technologies. Higher taxes at points of extraction and waste would encourage the use of recycled materials instead of new extraction for production, and support technologies that reduce waste, or divert by-products to productive use. This would be a way of more fully including in the cost of production the costs of what have been termed "externalities," a use of the commons that has often been assumed to be free. States in the U.S. are beginning to grapple with this issue as they consider severance taxes for natural gas extraction.

Removing hidden, or sometimes not so hidden, subsidies could even out the playing field in a way that would improve the chances of more sustainable technologies. If the oil industry were not subsidized so deeply, for example, alternative energy sources would be more competitive. If the subsidies were eliminated that the government makes to nuclear energy, by covering the costs of insurance and taking responsibility for "disposing" of wastes, the full cost of that form of energy would be clearer. If U.S. agribusiness were not so heavily subsidized by government, the small family farms (both here and abroad) would have a better chance. All of these issues are currently being discussed at high levels, but the lobbying by those industries that now gain from government subsidies is unrelenting and fierce.

Companies could be made responsible for disposal of the products they sell, or for their repair. Germany has taken the lead here. In 1991, they passed a law making producers responsible for product packaging after consumers discard it, launching what has come to be known as

Extended Producer Responsibility or ESR. ESR has become widely accepted in European Union governance, with producers required to take on increasing informative, liability, financial, physical, and long-term ownership responsibility for the products they market. Recycling rates have dramatically increased, and interest in zero-waste manufacturing has mushroomed.[77]

Advertising could be more closely regulated, more heavily taxed, or simply curtailed. More is possible, though corporate resistance would be enormous. We have examples in the U.S., in terms of tobacco, alcohol, and local restrictions on billboards, to build on. We can look to Scandinavia, where restrictions include a complete ban on advertising to children in some markets, restrictions on alcohol ads in most, limits on healthcare product promotions and absolutely no political or religious advertising on TV.[78]

Our choice at this fork in the road is a decisive one. Our current system of production, in terms of structure, governance and resource use, as it turns out, is a threat to both our cherished ideals of democracy and the future of human life on Earth. On the side of the future, however, is a rapidly growing awareness of this reality and a vast network of individuals, organizations, businesses and governments that are creating the pieces of a whole new way of producing in harmony with Earth.

CHAPTER SEVEN

The Commons, Collaborative Organizations and New Technologies
David Watkins

If we are to provide for the needs of all of the planet's people, for now and for the future, we will need new forms of organization and new technologies. At present there are enough material resources to satisfy the basic needs of all people, but existing economic and political structures are inadequate for fair distribution of these resources. Growth in the production of goods might be adequate to overcome the inadequacies of distribution, but current technologies are already exceeding the ecological capacity of the planet and are not sustainable. Our economic systems must function within the scope of the laws of thermodynamics. We must learn to live within our annual solar budget, with the planet's limited material resources and in a way that is integral and holistic. This chapter discusses governance of the commons, collaborative organizations, and new technologies that help to resolve the growth dilemma.

What are the Commons?

The commons are resources that we share. These resources include the land that we live on, the air that we breathe and the water that is necessary for life. They also include the cultures and institutions that make human civilization possible. The sharing is amongst people, with the entire biosphere, and with the future. The commons is about inclusive access. For example, land owned by the government, business, civic organizations, or individuals can be part of the commons if access is provided to everyone. There are two basic issues, 1) making sure that all appropriate resources are included in the commons and 2) how the commons are managed or governed for the common good.

The Tragedy of the Commons

"Therein is the tragedy. Each man is locked into a system that compels him to increase his herd without limit—in a world that is limited. Ruin

is the destination toward which all men rush, each pursuing his own best interest in a society that believes in the freedom of the commons."
—*Garrett Hardin*

Modern focus on the commons began in a negative way with Garret Hardin's 1968 essay, "The Tragedy of the Commons."[79] Hardin identified population increase as a problem for which there is no technical solution. Exponential growth on a planet with limited resources is not possible. In his search for the solution to the population problem, Hardin came to the popular concept of the "invisible hand" of Adam Smith, which was the idea that individuals acting in their own interest are led by an invisible hand to serve the public interest. In order to address the population issue, he constructed the tragedy of the commons to dispel the invisible hand of Adam Smith.

The scenario he used was that of a common pasture, open to all, upon which herdsmen grazed their stock. As rational beings each herdsman strives to maximize his individual gain. This works fine as long as there is a large enough commons for all of the herdsmen and all of their stock. As population increases beyond the carrying capacity of the common pasture, Hardin stated that there are only three possible outcomes: the government regulates the commons, the commons is privatized, or freedom in the commons leads inevitably to it being overgrazed and destroyed.

Many took Hardin's analysis to establish that the only way to save the commons was to enclose and privatize it. Others took it as establishing the need for additional government regulation and control, if the commons was to be saved. We will explore other possibilities. Our concerns go beyond those of population growth and extend to the need to nurture the planet, all its life now and for the future.

Governing the Commons

Governing common pool resources

On the positive side, the work of Elinor Ostrom, who won the 2009 Nobel Prize in Economics, offers a more appealing option in which the commons is governed by a complex of cooperative agencies, composed of the users themselves, determining the rules of engagement with the common resources. Ostrom establishes that commons can be successfully self-organized and self-managed over very long periods. She points out that the distinctions between public, private and commons are not as clear as is often assumed. Institutions for collective action evolve in diverse ways. She advocates a polycentric approach.

Ostrom and her group at the University of Indiana have studied many examples of governance of the commons worldwide.[80]

Ostrom focused on management of a form of the commons known as a "common pool resource" (CPR), which is a natural or human resource system that a number of individuals use, but it is too big and expensive for one individual to own and manage. CPRs are subtractable, that is, if one person uses too much, there is not enough available for other users. Not all commons are CPRs, so the governing systems that Ostrom describes may or may not apply to other commons.

Ostrom explains that both those who advocate governmental control of the commons, and those who conclude, as Hardin did, that the only solution is to privatize the commons, "accept as a central tenet that institutional change must come from outside and be imposed on the individuals affected. ... Instead of there being a single solution to a single problem, I argue that many solutions exist to cope with many different problems. Instead of presuming that optimal institutional solutions can be designed easily and imposed at low cost by external authorities, I argue that getting the institutions right is a difficult, time-consuming, conflict-invoking process."[81]

In her study of long-enduring, self-organized, and self-governed CPRs, Ostrom looks at the management of common grazing areas in Switzerland and Japan, and at the management of irrigation systems in Spain and the Philippines. The youngest set of these institutions has endured for over 100 years and the oldest for over 1,000 years. For our purposes the existence of such long-enduring self-organized and self-governed commons argues forcefully against Hardin's conclusion that commons must be either privatized, managed by the state, or face self-destruction.

After establishing that commons can be successfully managed over long periods of time, Ostrom took a closer look at what makes these self-governing organizations work over centuries. Her group also analyzed unsuccessful attempts to manage the commons to see what did not work. The following are several of their observations, which are useful in how we think about institutions, organization, governance, how change occurs, and for an understanding of how we can manage our commons:

- Successful institutions managing the commons are often hybrids, combining private and public institutions because a competitive market is itself a public good;

- The right to organize must be supported by the government or other outside controlling entities;

- Governance of the commons must be by the users themselves or those accountable to the users;

- Self-governing organizations worked only when resources and user boundaries were clearly defined;

- All users must have equal access and status;

- Sanctions and punishments must be appropriate to the offense with allowances for emergency situations; and

- Rapid access to low-cost conflict-resolution services is necessary.[82]

Ostrom makes it clear that commons can be successfully governed. There are options beyond private sector enclosure or state control. There is no simple formula for how we manage a CPR. Circumstances vary from CPR to CPR and within a CPR over time. Adjustments in how they are governed are often necessary. She provides us with an understanding of how institutions evolve to make governance of the commons possible.

Other approaches to governing the commons

Some look at the commons as a third sector, an addition to the public and private sectors. Others consider it a part of the fourth or "for-benefit" sector, with the other sectors being the public (government), private (business), and social (non-profit, non-governmental). "The defining characteristic of all Fourth Sector organizations is that they integrate social and environmental aims with business approaches. Some Fourth Sector organizations go further by embodying features like inclusive governance, transparent reporting, fair compensation, environmental responsibility, community service, and contribution of profits to the common good."[83]

These categories are not all that distinct. Government provides the context within which a business is formed. New hybrid models are being developed where businesses are designed to further social and environmental goals in addition to their need to make a profit. For-benefit corporations are being formed for the express purpose of managing common resources for the common good. For example, Charodic Commons is incorporated in Illinois as a "non-profit membership corporation." The term "charodic" means a system that combines both chaos and order. Their website invites people to become "owning members" and participate in initiatives that govern common resources. As of August 13, 2012, there were 862 members participating in 106 initiatives.[84]

Another approach is the "industrial ecology" approach. The International Society for Industrial Ecology "facilitates communication among scientists, engineers, policymakers, managers, and advocates who are interested in better integrating environmental concerns with economic activities."[85]

Reclaiming the Commons

The subtitle of Peter Barnes' book, *Capitalism 3.0,* indicates his solution to our current situation: *A Guide to Reclaiming the Commons.* As co-founder and former president of Working Assets Money Fund, Barnes believes that initiative should be rewarded with profits, but he is also concerned that profit-seeking institutions cause pollution, waste, inequality, anxiety, and confusion regarding the purpose of life. Governments tend to be controlled by corporations; so they cannot protect the interests of the people, the biosphere, or the future from the negative tendencies of markets.[86]

Over time private property and corporations have eroded the commons. Even as the enclosure of the commons through private property advanced relentlessly, costs were externalized from the private sector to the commons in various forms of pollution, social disorder, and waste. In the Capitalism 1.0 of a gathering and hunting society, the commons was everywhere. In the current Capitalism 2.0, the private sector and profits are nearly the only game in town. Barnes proposes Capitalism 3.0, a new set of institutions that run on two systems: "one geared to maximize private profit, the other to preserving and enhancing common wealth." He proposes a variety of new property rights, birthrights, and institutions that will extend and protect the commons, a "series of eco-system trusts that protect air, water, forests, and habitats."

There already exist many trusts of this nature that are effective within their scope. Land Trusts have existed for more than 2,000 years and were mostly used to hide the true ownership of the land. Since the twentieth century, however, land trusts have been used in the U.S. to conserve land by including a conservation easement to preserve land for perpetuity. The Community Land Trust (CLT) model was created over 30 years ago to provide affordable housing. Consistent with

Native American and other indigenous philosophies, the land in a CLT is viewed as common heritage. Title to the land is held by a non-profit that manages the land for the community. The land cannot be sold but can be used for housing, production of food, or other commercial uses for the common good. The Institute for Community Economics maintains a revolving fund that makes loans to community-based non-profit organizations, community land trusts, and other non-profit organizations involved in land trusts.[87]

Barnes proposes that similar trusts be developed to govern our air, water, and the sea. He argues that our economic system is rigged by mal-distributed property. "But how can we spread property ownership without taking property from some and giving it to others? The answer lies in the commons—wealth that already belongs to everyone. By propertizing (without privatizing) some of that wealth, we can make everyone a property owner."[88] Barnes details the limits of government and privatization, and proposes a reinvented commons as a solution.

Our current economic system clearly creates poverty and income inequality. The negative consequences of these for the entire society and for the economy are difficult to overestimate. Comparing nations and comparing the 50 states in the U.S., Quakers Richard Wilkerson and Kate Pickett make clear that income inequality has a large negative impact across more than a dozen social categories, including physical and mental health, education, and violence. Societies that are more equal do better by every measure considered, including economics, health, happiness, and longevity.[89]

Open Source Everything

Robert David Steele expresses the commons in terms of "opensource culture," which is analogous to the computer software development culture that has been open to all, rather than contained within a for-profit business. Steele is adamant that what is needed is a shift from top-down to bottom-up organization. Steele analyzes the human organization of the previous millennium, which was characterized by control from above with unilateral, non-consultative decision-making, predatory capitalism, increasing hierarchy, hoarding, and other acts of greed and insensitivity.[90]

He looks forward to the new millennium of restored human community and advocates open source sharing involving a variety of organizational conceptions, such as transparency, integrity, trust, holistic thinking and justice, with decision-making that is "multicultural, deeply appreciative of diversity, replete with integrity, and very much bottom up, harnessing the distributed intelligence of all."[91]

In the new millennium, Steele says that we are developing a network capable of connecting all individuals to all information all the time, which has the potential to strip the power from "rule by secrecy" hierarchies. Ultimately, this new operating system will be more effective and efficient, serving all. It will also be autonomous from governments and corporations.

Networked information in Steele's view can circumvent the negative aspects of governments and corporations. The expansion of transparency, truth, and trust across all boundaries through hybrid networks can provide flexible governance without government being in charge. Steele sees this leading to a new stage of human consciousness.

These connection enable a new ideal form of consciousness that Steele calls "Panarchy," which others have called the "Global Brain,"[92] the "Noosphere,"[93] or "Web 4.0."[94] He describes "panarchy" as "an ideal condition in which every individual would be connected to all relevant information and able to participate in every decision of interest to them, from local to global. Panarchy thus represents direct democracy within a nonhierarchical, open-source context."[95]

Open source is about sharing, the key feature of the commons. Steele takes sharing, collaboration, and cooperation to the extreme. It is by connecting all of the planet's people with all of the available information that we maximize our utilization of human intelligence and our wealth.

Networks as Emerging Commons

Yochai Benkler is concerned that there has been an excessive enclosure of the intellectual commons in recent years. He uses open source software as a prime example of how "social production" can transform markets and enhance our freedom. Networked peer-to-peer production is transforming businesses and creating a new intellectual commons. IBM amassed the largest number of patents of any company from 1993 to 2004. In 2000, virtually all of IBM's revenues came from patent-based sources. In 2003, approximately 60 percent of their revenues were described as "Linux-related services."[96]

The commons of Benkler's networks is very different from the CPRs that Ostrom examines. Appropriation from the Internet to share information, knowledge, and culture does not deplete its value, but more often enhances it. Open sharing is essential for the advance of human welfare, justice and freedom. From the perspective of the creation of an ecologically integrated economy that meets the needs of all of the planet's people and the protection of the global ecosystems, the networked information economy has much to offer.

Entropy and Empathy

A number of authors have discussed economic growth, the depletion of natural resources, and the development of a new economy grounded in principles that are central to the physical sciences and to ecology. These principles are closely related to the concept of the commons and the need for restoration of the commons, even though the terminology is not the same.

The first law of thermodynamics, the law of conservation, states that energy in the universe is never created nor destroyed. Although the energy in the universe remains constant, it is continually changing form. This change in form is always in one direction, from available to unavailable. According to the second law of thermodynamics, sometimes known as the law of entropy, energy always flows in one direction, from hot to cold, concentrated to dispersed, and from ordered to disordered. There are three kinds of thermodynamic systems; open, partially closed, and isolated. Open systems exchange both energy and matter; partially closed systems exchange energy but little matter; and closed systems exchange neither energy nor matter. The planet Earth is a partially closed system; it receives a steady stream of energy from the sun, but very little matter from any other system.

Jeremy Rifkin traces the role that entropy has played in the collapse of previous civilizations. He finds an "inescapable relationship between increasing energy throughput and a rising entropy debt." Two hundred years of burning coal, oil, and natural gas has released massive amounts of carbon dioxide into Earth's atmosphere, viewed by some as pollution and by others as a degradation of the atmospheric commons. In Rifkin's view, it is an entropic debt that has come due in the form of potentially disastrous climate change. What we need is an economic system that considers the reality of entropy, one that is budgeted on our annual solar income. Rifkin traces the growth of empathy accompanying resource depletion over the course of human civilization.[97]

> *"At the very core of the human story is the paradoxical relationship between empathy and entropy. Throughout history new energy regimes have converged with new communications revolutions and*

68

created ever more complex societies. More technologically advanced civilizations, in turn, have brought diverse people together, heightened empathic sensitivity, and expanded human consciousness. But these increasingly more complicated milieus require more extensive energy use and speed us toward resource depletion."[98]

Rifkin argues that government has a large role to play in jump-starting a third industrial revolution. Governments played large roles in both the first and second industrial revolutions. This is not to suggest that governments would control the revolution. Renewable energy is the primary element of the transition to the new industrial paradigm. Renewable energy tends to be widely distributed and with Rifkin's five pillar approach it would be distributed through Internet-like networks. The organization of energy distribution would be far less centralized than is the case today. Rifkin sees this as a move toward distributed capitalism, to be accompanied by a lateralization of power.

The Third Industrial Revolution (TIR) is our path away from the entropic abyss. Rifkin sees the emerging TIR as consisting of five pillars, which must develop simultaneously and in an integrated manner.[99]

1) Shifting to renewable energy;

2) Transforming the building stock of every continent into micro-power plants to collect renewable energies on site;

3) Deploying hydrogen and other storage technologies in every building and throughout the infrastructure to store intermittent energies;

4) Using Internet technology to transform the power grid of every continent into an energy-sharing intergrid that acts just like the Internet; and

5) Transitioning the transport fleet to electric plug-in and fuel cell vehicles that can buy and sell electricity in a smart continental interactive power grid.

With the TIR, Rifkin sees a move to distributed capitalism and a collaborative economy. The partial shift from markets to networks changes our business orientation. Adding value to the network does not diminish one's own stock, but appreciates everyone's holdings. Self-interest gives way to the common good and proprietary information is less effective than that which is openly shared. The open-source commons will thrive. The TIR changes not just how we use energy; it reorients the economy and permits restoration of the commons.

In 2007, the European Union bought into the five-pillar approach to the TIR as conceptualized by Rifkin. Cities as diverse as Monaco, Rome, San Antonio, and Utrecht have collaborated with Rifkin to develop TIR master plans.

The TIR is not something that will happen overnight. Rifkin projects that it will take four or five decades, as did the first and second industrial revolutions. The positive side is that it will create millions of jobs over these decades. It is a process that is already emerging. It is critical that we hasten the pace and perfect the vision.

Rifkin is not the only one to recognize the entropic problem relative to business and technology as usual. Buckminster Fuller's comprehensive, anticipatory design approach to technology is in many ways similar to Rifkin's five-tier approach.[100] Herman Daly brought attention to the role of ecological science and the laws of thermodynamics in economics.[101]

In their book, *Natural Capitalism,* Hawken, Lovins, and Lovins use a holistic and integral approach to face the issue of entropy. Their premise is that at the beginning of the industrial revolution there was an abundance of natural resources and a shortage of human labor. Now we have a major shortage of many of our most critical natural resources and over half of the planet's people do not have meaningful jobs. By applying whole systems design principles, we can conserve natural resources in every industrial sector in ways that engage more human labor, thus enhancing the value of labor and eliminating some of the economic costs that are associated with poverty and income disparity. Hawken *et al* assert that the issue of limited resources can be solved through market forces alone.[102]

A complementary approach to facing the problem of entropy and the growth dilemma is found in the book *Factor Five: Transforming the Global Economy through 80% Improvements in Resource Productivity.* In this highly technical book, the authors show that with existing technologies resource productivity can be increased by a factor of five for large portions of every industrial sector. Engaging these technologies could reduce resource consumption and waste ,even as we meet the needs of the planet's increasing population and of those who now do without.[103]

Protecting, Restoring, and Evolving the Commons?

Proposed here is an approach to institutions and organizations that would be aimed at fulfilling the real needs of all of the planet's people, the planet, and the future. It involves cooperation and collaboration among businesses, governments, civic and commons-governing organizations, and individual citizens.

The boundaries amongst these various forms are not as distinct as we often tend to think. As Ostrom reminds us, the private-rights system is a public institution dependent on public instrumentalities for its very existence. Government policy can enhance or destroy the commons. Civic organizations can look very much like businesses, and triple-bottom-line businesses can be as beneficial as other forms of organization.

Emerging communications and networking technologies enable people and institutions to interact in ways that were not possible previously. This in turn allows new ways of cooperation, sharing, and collaboration. Cooperation and collaboration are rapidly evolving as arts and sciences with the benefit of new enabling technologies.[104]

Businesses can play a positive role with regard to the commons. Sustainable and ecologically sensitive approaches can make businesses partners with commons-oriented organizations by giving full consideration to the environment and to social justice, even as businesses pursue reasonable profits.

Government has a vital role to play in creating new legal forms and institutions that foster the commons. It is unlikely that excessive business and corporate influence in government will end, but political pressure from civic and commons-governing organizations, along with private citizens and businesses with a conscience, can influence government to protect and restore the commons.

Civic and commons-governing organizations are faced with the prospect of having better information and tools for collective action. Hawken describes what he calls "the world's largest movement," tens of thousands of organizations around the globe that are working largely independent of each other for similar issues of the environment and social justice.[105]

From the perspective of complex and general evolutionary theory, there are shifts in the behaviors of whole systems that we cannot predict or control. However, we are not helpless in the face of these changes. As complexity increases within a system, emergent change is more likely. We can predict some aspects of these changes, even if others are nonlinear and unpredictable.

The emerging communications and networking technologies are adding complexity to the planet's social systems. It is likely that many of our social institutions will not be adequate to our new situation. A global economic system, based on continuous exponential material growth and on the excessive consumption of natural resources, is clearly not sustainable. Just what will emerge to replace our existing social systems is not clear.

An interdisciplinary group of quantum physicists and biologists have developed a field theory of evolution describing an underlying evolutionary process in which there is an intelligent field that some would identify as God or Spirit. In this view, evolution is not guided by random chance but is supplied with a variety of spiritual forms. In the beginning was the Word. The enfolded implicate order unfolds through the evolutionary process into our everyday world, the explicate order. The evolutionary process moves towards greater consciousness, cooperation, empathy, and love. We all play a role in this unfolding. Our conscious choices, both individually and collectively, influence the track of planetary evolution.[106]

CHAPTER EIGHT

An Ecologically Integrated Economy
Ed Dreby

In "Earth as a Spaceship" in 1965, Kenneth Boulding said that humanity must "face the fact that we are a biological system living in an ecological system," and our survival will depend on "developing symbiotic relationships of a closed-cycle character with all the other elements and populations of the world of ecological systems."[107] Subsequently, ecological economist Herman Daly has devoted his career to spelling out the implications of this prediction for economic theory.[108] What follows is an attempt to provide a simple explanation of what Boulding probably had in mind when he said that "all [our] major problems are still unsolved."[109]

The challenge of developing an economy that functions within ecological limits will hinge on producing better with less and changing the general attitude that "more is better" to one based upon "enough." What economic mechanisms can be established to assure that a limited flow of physical resources is used in progressively better ways? What can be done to prevent a systemic demand for exploiting more resources than Earth's bio-productivity can sustain?

Whether one thinks our best way forward at this time is to focus on the kind of economic growth we need, or to advocate for systemic change to accommodate compassionate retreat, the most basic findings of both physics and biology point toward the future need for an ecologically integrated economy. How might this come about?

One way to approach this challenge is to revise our collective understanding of capital, efficient allocation, productivity, money, and some of our other basic cultural assumptions and expectations.

Capital in an Ecologically Integrated Economy

In traditional economic theory, there are three factors of production: land, labor, and capital. "Capital" refers to what the economy manufactures for the purpose of producing and distributing goods and services. As the financial industry developed, the term "financial capital" was introduced to distinguish it from what was then called "real capital" or "physical capital." As used in economic theory, "investment" means "to use economic surplus to increase the economy's real capital to produce more and better goods and services." But in common parlance, "capital" has come to mean one's surplus money, and investing is using savings to make more money.

Ecological economists define "capital" as a physical stock that can provide the economy with a flow of useful resources. They refer to the capital that provides a flow of products as "manufactured capital," which is similar to the traditional economic term, "real capital." They distinguish that from "natural capital" that provides a flow of physical resources. Natural capital is similar to the traditional economic term "land." For ecological economists, natural capital is fundamental because all manufacturing requires natural capital, and the flow of resources it can provide depends on conserving and enhancing the quality and quantity of its capital stocks, such as, fertile fields and healthy forests.[110]

Corporations now refer to the skills of their workforce as "human capital" and to their patented technologies as "intellectual capital." Many ecologically oriented economists now refer to the values, expectations, and interactive skills that any organization or community needs to function as "social capital."

In *Ecological Economics,* Daly and Farley detail the distinctive ecological characteristics of different types of biotic and abiotic stocks and flows, including these particulars. Harvesting a renewable stock at a faster rate than its regenerative capacity reduces the productivity of the stock and eventuates in its demise. A sustainable economy would include the development of a renewable substitute as a cost of harvesting a non-renewable stock.[111]

Our existing system is over-producing manufactured capital to provide financial returns for the few. Our institutions to maintain and enhance human and social capital are being starved, and institutions with a primary purpose of maintaining and enhancing natural capital are effectively non-existent. Humans are part of nature, and the attitude that humans are separate from nature is a basic problem, because it leads us to the erroneous conclusion that we do not have to obey the laws of nature.

An ecologically integrated economy would recognize that all economic activity originates with resources drawn from stocks of natural capital: sunlight, soil, and water at a minimum. The flows of these resources, while not fixed, are limited by the quality, scale, and capacity for renewal of the stocks from which they are drawn. We must trust that ecologically integrated economies will be able to help restore and enhance Earth's bio-capacity, for in the long run, humanity is entirely dependent on Earth's bio-productivity. The biosphere will not get any larger.

How Might an Ecologically Integrated Economy Function Differently?

Our understanding of efficient allocation would change from producing as many goods and services that markets demand at the least possible cost, to using a limited flow of physical resources for maintaining and enhancing all capital stocks: natural, human, social, and manufactured. Our understanding of productivity must change from how much dollar value a worker adds to a product, to how long a resource flow from a capital stock can be sustained, and how much use value a material or energy resource provides in its economic life cycle.

An ecologically integrated economy would use non-renewable resources as sparingly and carefully as possible; so their stocks could be drawn as long as possible, while renewably based substitutes are developed. Harvesting of renewable resources would not compromise their capacity for renewal. Ecosystems would be carefully protected so the harvesting of resources and benefits from ecosystem services can continue indefinitely. In an ecologically integrated economy the limited flow of energy and material resources would be allocated in the best possible way to maintain and enhance all its capital: natural, human, social, and manufactured.

All manufactured stocks would be designed to last as long as possible, to be repaired as readily as possible, to have their parts re-used as much as possible, and to have their materials recycled as completely as possible. The same applies to all manufactured products. The by-products of manufacturing would be cycled forward into other forms of production. The "waste" of one process becomes the feedstock of another. All the economy's machinery, for essentials like construction and farming, and non-essentials like lawn care and recreation, would be designed to use the optimal combination of human, electrical, and other forms of energy. Products of all kinds would be distributed as much as possible in bulk, using re-usable containers for loose and liquid items, and as little energy as possible for transport.

The current problem of managing economic surplus would be guided by the need to allocate a limited flow of resources to maintain and enhance all the society's capital stocks at optimal scales. Because their productivity depends on the relative stability of Earth's bio-physical cycles, all economic activity would be guided by the need to re-stabilize Earth's carbon, hydrologic, nitrogen, and other biophysical cycles, ending the release of all substances in quantities that are damaging to the commonwealth of life.

The current problem of providing full employment would be solved by recognizing that making effective use of everyone's personal energy will necessarily be part of an ecologically integrated economy's energy mix. The idea of replacing humans with machines (whenever profitable for investors) will not survive the imperative of living within Earth's bio-capacity.

Money in an Ecologically Integrated Economy?

Modern money, unlike real capital, does not obey the laws of physics and biology, and we get into trouble when we ignore this. A for-profit monetary system based on interest-bearing debt confuses real wealth with debt, which is an abstract human invention. As Herman Daly and John Cobb explain,

> *"The positive physical quantity [of] two pigs represents wealth that can be seen and touched. But minus two pigs, debt, is an imaginary negative magnitude with no physical dimension. One could as easily have a thousand negative pigs as two. ... Compound interest or exponential growth of negative pigs presents no problem. But exponential growth of positive pigs soon leads to bedlam and ruin."[112]*

Yet there is a problem with the exponential growth of negative pigs when we try to breed enough positive pigs to equate the two. Or when we harvest fish or trees faster than the stocks can regenerate in order to prevent a debt from increasing.

Figuratively speaking, we are already beginning to experience bedlam from trying to maintain the equation of positive with negative pigs. Will we manage to avoid ruin? Which poses the greater threat: war, climate disruption, peak everything, or negative pigs?

76

According to economic theory, money serves three functions: a medium of exchange, a standard of account, and a store of value. Money loaned at interest is actually serving a fourth function: a means of accumulation of financial wealth for the lender, and as a lien on future earnings of the borrower.

A dollar bill, or a Federal Reserve Note, is a form of debt, a promise to pay the bearer on demand whatever the dollar or note will buy. But when the money is in the form of a bank check drawn on an account created by a loan, the borrower is obligated to pay interest to the bank as well as to repay the loan itself. And under current law, the government must pay interest on the bonds that secure the Federal Reserve's Notes.

When virtually the entire money supply is created by interest-bearing debt, before any goods are sold, there are creditors with a prior claim to some of those goods. With this kind of system, the entire productive economy must either keep producing more or the productive sector will keep ending up with less than it had before.

Paying interest on almost the entire money supply has no inherent benefit except to its beneficiaries, especially when the need to do this comes from an abstract legal invention. As Henry Ford reportedly said, "It is well enough that people of the nation do not understand our banking and monetary system, for if they did I believe there would be a revolution before tomorrow morning."[113]

So what are the alternatives?

The federal government does not need to delegate the issuing of its national currency to a for-profit banking system when it already has an institution, the Fed, that could be authorized to issue national interest-free currency. This would enable the Fed to adjust the size of the money supply to serve the general welfare, rather than having to do this by attending to the welfare of the financial establishment. It would also greatly reduce the need for the federal government to borrow money and pay interest to private lenders.

Banks would then have a 100% reserve requirement, and could only lend the money they have on deposit. It would have a major effect of reducing speculation in financial markets. It would eliminate the monetary instability created by the current system's multiplier effect, and enable the Fed to manage the money supply during a recession. This is why many of the ecologically oriented critics of the current economic system, whatever proposals they have to provide for global, regional, and local well-being, call for an end to fractional reserve banking.

Congresman Dennis Kucinich has introduced a bill, HR 2990, to reform the monetary system in this way. HR 2990 is modeled on a proposal for monetary reform called the "Fisher Plan" that was endorsed by a group of prominent economists and submitted to President FDR in 1939.

A banking system, or some other means like credit unions, would certainly be needed to aggregate household savings and lend them for investment so they are not withdrawn from circulation. Because a financial system charged with this responsibility would be essentially a public service for administering the circulation of the national currency, it should be structured as a non-profit, public service business.

Interest would be converted to a fee-for-service structure that would supply the institutional income needed to operate the service. Credit unions already provide one form of this model. Designing a banking and financial system that uses market mechanisms and rewards enterprise for allocating investment wisely to maintain and enhance all capital stocks will be one of the challenges for our most ingenious economists and policy professionals.

An economy certainly cannot function within ecological limits if the tremendous expansion of compound interest dominates the entire monetary system. It is perhaps ironic that many, like me, who are concerned about the role of compound interest in driving unbridled economic expansion and speculation, are also living on retirement income that comes from compound interest. This is also true of the endowments of many institutions to which we are loyal.

Private pension plans and retirement accounts, however regulated and managed, are owned by individuals and invested in the financial system with all of the compromises and risks this entails. In contrast, social security is a commitment by society as a whole to provide income for retirees from the earnings of the current workforce, their children and grandchildren. This can be viewed as a form of income redistribution; but it can also be understood as a way that highly mobile market economies can fulfill a moral obligation that used to be met by families and communities in household economies.

An ecologically integrated economy will require a reversal in the current trend toward individual retirement accounts, and to make social

78

security primary in our thinking, both for the good of the individual and the well-being of society.

Many questions have been raised by monetary critics about the relationship between our national currency and the economic well-being of communities, regions, sectors and states; and also about its relationship to the currencies, economies, and well-being of other nations and peoples. Various local currencies have been or are in use, and global models have been proposed to provide income for retirees from the earnings of the current workforce, their children and grandchildren. These options will be an essential part of designing a comprehensive monetary and financial system for a world of ecologically integrated economies.[115]

A Critical Choice

In order to devise an ecologically integrated economy, society must make a fundamental ethical choice about what the values of freedom and equality mean, and how they should be manifested in the economy and the culture.[116] Does freedom mean the right to do whatever you please that you can get away with? Do people have an equal right to be protected from harm caused by the actions of other people? Should corporations, whose only purpose is to make money, be treated sometimes as a person and other times not as a person, depending on whether or not it helps them make money?

In a cowboy economy that presumes an illimitable Earth, the inherent conflict between the values of freedom and equality can be ignored by a dominant population for a limited time, as occurred when Europeans came to the Americas. But if we truly realize that Earth is a spaceship, a stark choice must be made between promoting the well-being of humanity as a whole and permitting the self-aggrandizement of an elite class. Friends testimonies witness to an ecologically integrated economy that is egalitarian and inclusive, one that promotes the well-being of the whole.

In order to maintain and enhance its human and social capital, an ecologically integrated economy would have provisions for enabling all its members to contribute to the enrichment of the whole, as well as to their own well-being and enrichment. In an ecologically integrated economy, two prominent features of every young person's education would be to demonstrate a clear understanding of what a sustainable human-Earth relationship requires, and to learn by engaging in community service.

An ecologically integrated economy would require more jobs that are more labor-intensive. It would be easy to find enough useful work for everyone who needs a job, and make the work meaningful, if that is one of the economy's priorities. A system for properly valuing and widely sharing the sometimes unpleasant maintenance work of our physical and social environments would be built into an ecologically integrated economy.

The expectation that everyone contributes to the well-being of the whole applies not only to those we classify as elderly and disabled, but also to those who violate society's more extensive and intrusively enforced rules. How can restorative justice become a reality? How can the penal system have effective incentives to provide for their inmates' fundamental rights of bodily and psychological integrity, and for opportunities to contribute to their own and society's well-being and enrichment?

What Must We Give up to Keep What We Value Most?

In an ecologically integrated economy, providing a basic livelihood for everyone inevitably would mean limiting how much of many things any individual can use. It would mean revising what can and cannot be owned by whom, and what an "owner" is required to do and prohibited from doing. The idea of a comprehensive and permanent system of rationing seems repugnant and unworkable by current standards. Yet this is exactly what markets do, based on the amount of money people have at their disposal. Boulding and Daly are both strong believers in the uses of well-designed markets.

Devising ways for using markets to allocate and distribute the fruits of a limited flow of resources with wisdom and fairness would perhaps be the only way for an inclusive ecologically integrated economy to function without exceeding Earth's bio-capacity. Fair distribution will be made all the more challenging because people's legitimate needs are most certainly unequal, and the same limited flow of resources that provides goods and services for its people, *i.e.*, its human and social capital, must also be allocated to maintain and enhance its natural and manufactured capital.

There must be a systematic means to limit the size of the population if it does not occur by individuals' choices. Either the death rate must be managed according to the birth rate, or the birth rate must be managed according to the death rate. Otherwise the population will become self-limiting in an unpleasant and dangerous Malthusian fashion.[117]

Boulding offended other Friends by proposing that population be managed by giving all adults the same number of tradeable "birth certificates" they could use to have children or sell to another would-be parent. He proposed this market mechanism as the fairest way to preserve a degree of reproductive choice. He insisted some method of population control would be needed because without one, sooner or later, too many people would use too many resources and our spaceship would fail us as a self-renewing system, which is now happening.[118]

How Do We Get There from Here?

With the lens we now use to view the economy, getting from here to an ecologically integrated economy seems utterly impossible. Yet getting there, or someplace like it, is the essence of our unsolved problems. Humans are inventive; necessity is the mother of invention; and we are soon apt to be faced with many more urgent necessities.

There are two distinct, though inseparable, aspects to establishing an ecologically integrated economy. One is to re-design the economic system itself. The far greater challenge is to transform the core beliefs and values of the consumer culture created by the needs of the growth economy.

Designing an ecologically integrated economy would be a relatively tangible task because most of its aspects can be measured numerically. Many economic policies and practices that worked well in the past have been forgotten or distorted. Ecological economists and their allies are gaining experience with alternative models that are not widely known.

For example, it is hard for most people to imagine that our monetary and financial systems could be very different than what they are. Yet many past monetary systems were quite different; many alternatives are being explored; and it should be quite feasible to create a monetary and financial system for an ecologically integrated economy.[119]

In spite of inevitable distortions and unintended consequences, an economic system that intentionally adapts to ecological and social realities can be continuously modeled, monitored, and modified until its parameters, incentives, and feedbacks function as intended.

To allocate a sustainable flow of resources to maintain and enhance all capital stocks for the well-being and enrichment of all the members of the society, our entire economic establishment must be induced to consider:

- how the rights and responsibilities of ownership and management can be revised,

- how market mechanisms, economic incentives, and the profit motive can be redirected, and

- what metrics and feedback mechanisms are needed.

The good news is that electronic technologies that helped create the excesses of our financial markets can also be used to manage the complexities of very different accounting systems and market mechanisms.

A Far Greater Challenge

Shaping cultural values and behavior is a much less tangible enterprise than designing an economy's institutions, regulations, and incentives. Social scientists disagree about how much culture shapes economic behavior and institutions, and how much economic incentives shape culture.[120]

But it is clear that since the 1920s, and especially since the 1980s, the increasingly contrived and targeted language and imagery of media programming and advertising has bent the popular culture's core beliefs, values, and motivations to the needs of the growth economy in general, and its market-fundamentalist version in particular.[106]

The following current cultural trends would be problematic at best, and perhaps prohibitive, for an ecologically integrated economy. So changing them would be necessary.

The equating of wants with needs and the self-fulfilling assumption that needs are insatiable.

The idea that this is a fundamental characteristic of human nature is contradicted by evidence from many other cultures, the massive expenditures from advertising and marketing to promote consumption, and even by economic theory's "law of diminishing returns."

The manufactured perception that one's possessions and material affluence are the mark of social standing and personal fulfillment.

Transforming the culture's beliefs about personal well-being, social relationships, and spiritual fulfillment is perhaps the most basic requirement for enabling an ecologically integrated economy to succeed.

The persistence of discrimination based on race, ethnicity, class, gender, and sexual orientation, and the entrenched practice of blaming the victims of discrimination for its effects.

This residue from humanity's tribal past would be an anathema in an egalitarian ecologically integrated economy, in which the society needs to enhance the contributions of its social capital to the best possible extent.

The persistence of religious fundamentalism, and its rejection of the scientific method as a source of continuing revelation about physical reality and moral precepts.

The scientific method has enabled us to realize that we are only one of many species in an intricate and miraculous web of life. To what extent can an ecologically integrated economy accommodate traditional, tribal-like beliefs and self-serving manipulations that contradict vital truths about the human-Earth relationship?

The increasing prevalence of dishonesty in advertising, business, finance, politics, and the mass media.

An ecologically integrated economy must be based on a society's right to expect its members to be truthful at all times.

The immoral practices of certain individuals and corporations to corrupt government with money, and then to attack government for the incompetence and corruption that results.

This exploits people and planet in ways that only the establishment of an ecologically well-informed, democratic government can restrain and overcome.

Recourse to violence, the threat of violence, and the right of access to weapons, as a means of personal and societal protection and security.

"We cannot afford unrestrained conflict, and we almost certainly cannot afford national sovereignty in an unrestricted sense."[122]

For an ecologically integrated economy to work, the most daunting challenge, perhaps, is to devise forms of local, national, and global governance, that, with the consent of the governed, impose sufficient limits on the human use of Earth.

These challenges illustrate the truth of Kenneth Boulding's warning that we must be made to realize humanity's major problems are still unsolved. The economic problems he described are still largely unrecognized, and some are hotly denied. He identified a few cultural trends as potential traps, but they have become much more pronounced since the 1960s.[123] The human population was less than half its current size, the specter of peak oil was far away, climate disruption was not yet on the horizon, corruption was much less acceptable, and ideological conflicts were far less entrenched.

An ecologically integrated economy would require a very different set of rights and responsibilities than wealthy Americans currently regard as self-evident entitlements. They would include rights of society and the commonwealth of life, and the responsibilities of individuals to honor those rights. They would involve very different interpretations of rights and responsibilities relating to speech, property, and privacy.

In view of the nation's current ideological polarization and the influence of money and finance in politics, it may be much more likely for an ecologically integrated economy to emerge from the collapse of the growth economy than by a bumpy transition. But the prospects for an ecologically integrated economy to eventually succeed will be greatly enhanced if there is a clearer understanding of why the growth economy has led to a pending convergence of ecological disruption, resource scarcity, and unmanageable debt, and how an ecologically integrated economy would need to be different.[31] A clearer understanding is a source of hope.

"Hope is not the conviction that something will turn out well, but the certainty that something makes sense, regardless of how it turns out."   *—Vaclav Havel[124]*

"I think hope is a verb; it is something you do, a practice.... Hope is real, but only when individuals exercise it, practice it." —Joe Volk[125]

"Hope is grounded in the belief that God is at work, and that means that if human beings open themselves to God, "miracles" can happen. ... There is no guarantee that miracles will save humanity from terrible catastrophes. But we can hope that through them and beyond them God will work in and through those who are open to God's call to bring about something quite positive. In that sense, "another world is possible."   *—John B. Cobb[126]*

CHAPTER NINE

The Way Foward
Pamela Haines and Judy Lumb

Our hopes for the future begin with a clear understanding of the potential for an ecologically integrated economy. We must chart a way toward that future, working together for changes at all levels of society to help build a new creation that is inclusive of all and fits within the physical capacities of Earth.

This path calls for a radical change in our interactions with each other and Earth—from a focus on material goods to holistic well-being, from excess to sufficiency, exclusion to inclusion, competition to cooperation, pursuing privilege to serving the common good, pre-eminence of humanity to reverence for all life.

We know this change will be an incremental process. During a sustained and challenging period of transition, the building blocks of new ecologically integrated economies will have to exist side by side, often uneasily, with the old system of fossil-fuel-driven and profit-oriented expansion.

Everyone can be part of this process of creating a new future—an ecologically integrated economy—and there are roles to play on many levels: as individual consumers, producers and people of faith; as members of our local communities; as business-people, inventors, engineers and educators; and as engaged citizens.

As Individuals

There are many concrete steps we can take individually as responsible members of an economic community, most of which are already familiar to Quakers. We can consume less, with attention to minimizing waste and reducing our eco-footprint in our consumption, housing, energy, water, and transit choices, and buying more sustainable and local products. We can produce more, both in terms of food and goods, and in entertainment, care of the old and young, and education. We can repair and share rather than buying new, and think creatively about building our livelihoods from pieces. We can rethink our choices about where we keep our liquid assets and our investments, prioritizing local, cooperative and socially beneficial institutions. We can inform ourselves about the implications of new political or economic developments for an ecologically integrated economy, and play an active role as citizens.

Yet, for there to be any major shifts in our economic systems, we have to move beyond individual choices. A shift in awareness is required, an acknowledgment that we have no existence and no future separate from our ecosystem, a re-awakened sense of community and the interdependence we have with one another and all parts of God's creation. This shift calls for a vast cultural change, from the insatiable reach for "more" to a prosperity of "enough".

If we have made that shift ourselves, then we need to look around and see what we can do to help it spread. How can we model a Spirit-led, Earth-connected, and purpose-filled life, and share the values that undergird it with our friends, our neighbors, our colleagues, our children. How can we act on our faith more widely and speak up about what we know is true?

In Communities

We can help others take the practical steps that we have learned to take. We can use the model of the Friendly Households project to support others in our religious congregations or local communities to reduce our ecological footprints. We can gather groups, for a one-time forum or a series of meetings, to learn about the growth dilemma, about the imperative for a new ecologically integrated economy, and what we can do to help each other on the journey. Common Security Clubs provide one model; the Transition Town initiative is another powerful resource.

We can begin to learn about our own local economic and ecological systems: Who works at what, and spends where? What are the local sources of production of goods and services? What are the commons that we value—ecological, social and cultural? Where is our wealth? Mapping those systems and sources of common wealth is likely to lead to many ideas for ways to build local resilience. The process of working together, in itself, will help increase the sense of commonality and solid social attachment that is fundamental to a healthy economy.

Once we understand our local economies better, we can begin to develop strategies to support and strengthen them. Instead of depending upon influences from afar, communities can develop an awareness of local resources—the farmers, producers, employee-owned businesses, consumer and producer cooperatives, professionals, banks and credit unions already in their midst—and encourage local buying, banking and investment. This will increase support for local food systems and commerce, and encourage small businesses that are rooted in their communities and financed without stockholders.

Livelihoods can be rethought together, starting with awareness of local job producers and their potential to grow. A system of time banks can allow the exchange of value, including professional services, without money. The rebuilding of skills, development of skills-sharing networks, support for apprenticeships in local businesses, support for job sharing, and encouragement of reuse and recycle businesses, can all reduce dependence on external employers, strengthen local economies, and decrease the toll on the environment.

Communities can find opportunities to work together on local policies that impact the creation of ecologically integrated economies. One obvious opportunity is to rally together to oppose threats: big box stores squeezing out local competition, or corporate plans that threaten the commons. There may be steps to reclaim the commons that can be taken locally, or on a statewide level, to create policies that realign the tax base, claim governance of the local commons, and establish trusts to protect the air, water, forests, and habitats.

Other steps a community might take include supporting building and retrofitting for energy efficiency, encouraging public and cooperative financial institutions, and supporting for-benefit corporations. Once a community gains confidence in working together and deepens its pool of shared resources, it will have greater capacity to design other needed community projects cooperatively using local labor and resources instead of relying on external sources and going into debt.

There are dozens of possible ways to move forward to increase the resilience of local communities. Anything that facilitates a rich flourishing of local and regional culture, supports a healthy and engaged local government, builds open source systems, promotes a rebirth of social collaboration and cooperation, and restores our sense of oneness can be part of the solution.

In Business, Technology, Entrepreneurship and Education

Those who are involved in business, technology and entrepreneurship have unlimited opportunities to play a role in the transition to an ecologically integrated economy. For example, in the energy field, there is a crying need for micro-power plants that collect energy on site, development of on-site energy storage technologies, "intergrids" that share energy, green building innovations, a new generation of fuel-efficient cars, and the power grids to support them.

Technologies are needed in all areas of production that apply whole system design principles to conserve natural resources, replacing the linear model of extraction-production-waste with a circular model in which by-products of one process are inputs into another. New technologies need to be evaluated for their entire input of fuels and natural resources, and for their long-term contribution to, or potential undermining of, the common good. New products need to be designed for longevity, reliability, reparability, and recyclability, and our concepts of efficiency need to shift toward productive processes that use less finite resources and value job creation.

Current businesses can move forward in these ways. They can consider questions of how they are financed, how they are governed, how they procure, how they hire, and how they invest their profits, moving toward more responsiveness to, and reliance on, local resources. They can innovate in the creation of apprenticeship and job sharing systems. They can use their influence and resources to encourage the development of resilient local economies.

Educators can help make ecological understanding as basic as the three Rs, and include the principles involved in the creation of an ecologically integrated economy into a wide range of disciplines at the high school and college levels. They can play a role in the development of online resources and the education of community groups. They also have an important role in the expansion of open source education online.

National Policy and Legislation

Since specific economic and environmental policy initiatives at the federal level are unlikely to directly address the broad goals of creating an ecologically integrated economy, at least in the short term, it will be useful to have some principles in mind that can help guide our response to specific political proposals. As we consider proposed legislation or administrative initiatives, and choose areas in which to concentrate our outreach, education, and lobbying efforts, we must ask whether a proposal moves us toward our goals, or if it tends to protect and extend the status quo.

Policy Guidance

1) Does this proposal support the idea that basic resources are finite and must be governed for the public good?

2) Does it facilitate the full cost accounting for all human activities, goods, and services?

3) Does it limit the power of corporations that function only according to the profit motive and encourage for-benefit corporations that consider the triple bottom line of profit, people and planet?

4) Does it encourage the development of small businesses and cooperative enterprises?

5) Does it advance a living wage and strengthen a platform of basic income support?

6) Does it help to reduce great inequality and advance a better sharing of social and material resources?

7) Does it support an accurate measure of societal well-being to replace the current measures that are limited by the profit-making economic systems?

8) Does it support the creation of the national currency and the management of financial operations under not-for-profit, public interest control?

Global commons

For the preservation of our future, the global commons must be protected. Our common air, oceans, fresh water, and biota should be put into public trust. Our precious common wealth of finite material resources needs to be preserved for the common good and not subject to control of private ownership.

Official recognition of the rights of nature would establish an important foundation. Then we must promote full cost accounting for the use of material and energy resources for stock maintenance; this could be reflected in the price of the goods and services, or the tax structure might be used to pay these costs for the common good. A restructuring of our tax system toward higher taxing of depletion and pollution, for example, would encourage recycling of resources and discourage the extraction of our remaining fossil fuels.

Our cultural heritage and accumulated information are also global commons. We must reverse the current trend of making claims on knowledge, especially indigenous wisdom, and placing it into private ownership.

Wealth distribution and livelihood

The goal of a moral economy is to ensure livelihood, not to accumulate wealth. Resources and wealth should be distributed such that everyone can have a livelihood. Extreme wealth disparities damage both the wealthy and the poor, so there is a great need to reverse the trend of the transfer of wealth from the poor and middle classes to the wealthy. Initiating or increasing taxes on financial transactions would help to reverse this trend.

The tax structure can also be used to reduce unemployment by encouraging flexibility in the length of the work day or week, changing the concept of "full-time work." Job-sharing could also be encouraged by giving tax advantages for providing benefits to all employees.

Global wealth re-distribution between countries must also be encouraged. Greater regulation of capital mobility between countries would allow nations to prioritize building resilient economies and meeting their social needs. Encouraging local economies will require protection from standards-lowering competition from abroad, moving us away from globilization and fair trade.

One legislative initiative that would help to redistribute wealth is what has been called the "Robin Hood Tax" (HR 6411). Introduced by Keith Ellison of Minnesota as the Inclusive Security Act, HR 6411 provides for a specific tax on the trading of stocks, bonds, derivatives and currency, like a sales tax on Wall Street trading. If passed, a tiny tax of 0.005% to 0.5% would be imposed on the trade of stocks (equal to 50 cents on the purchase or sale of $100 worth of stock with lesser amounts on bonds and derivatives). This tax has the potential of raising up to $350 billion annually, money that could be used to meet human needs here in the U.S. and around the world. As this pamphlet goes to press in October, 2012, there is a coordinated campaign to lobby for the passage of HR 6311 with U.S. law-makers in their constituencies while they are on their 2012 election break.[127]

Production

Systems of production should be organized in a way that mini-mizes extraction, waste, and transport costs, and maximizes food access and durability of necessary goods, with systems of finance organized to support such production. The tax structure can be changed to reduce subsidies for fuel-intensive and environmentally damaging industries, tax at the point of extraction and waste, and encourage durability and recycling.

Prices of goods and services must more accurately reflect their true value and cost, including the cost of disposal, and producers should be held responsible for repair and recycling of whatever they produce.

In current U.S. legislation, the Farm Bill should end subsidies that benefit industrial agriculture and instead support community-based agriculture, local production, and financial institutions that serve their communities.

Governance

Democracy requires that governments freely elected by the people have the power to establish measures of common well-being, and restrain institutions that are no longer serving the common good or are threatening the future viability of life on Earth. An important organizing principle of governance is the concept of subsidiarity, that matters ought to be handled by the smallest, least centralized, and most accessible competent authority.

Corporations currently have enormous control over our lives through their involvement in the political process and the daily assault of commercial advertising. It is essential that we limit the power of corporations by limiting their influence on elections, curbing monopolies, and reclaiming the public right to reissue and revoke charters. If the airwaves were considered as commons, media and advertising could be more strictly regulated, and help to slow the tide of consumption through needs-creation.

Since our current monetary system is a basic driver of economic growth, we need policies that move away from a debt-based, profit-making system with fractional reserve banking and toward a monetary system that functions as a non-profit public service.

Representative Dennis Kucinich of Ohio has introduced a bill in the U. S. House of Representatives (HR 2990) that would prohibit banks from using debt to create money. It would end fractional reserve banking and give authority to the Department of Treasury, on behalf of Congress, to create U.S. money the national currency and put it into circulation. If this legislation were passed it would enable the government to create and spend debt-free money that would be used for infrastructure rebuilding for the next five years. Then the spending of debt-free money would be extended to healthcare and education. It is estimated that this debt-free spending on infrastructure alone would create seven million jobs.

As this pamphlet goes to press in October 2012, the 112th Congress is drawing to a close without any action on the Kucinich bill.[128]

Engaging the Powers

While it would be comforting to imagine that a change of this magnitude could happen by diligently working to build alternatives in our communities, and by sustained attention to lobbying at the national level, such a shift is not likely to occur without a struggle. There needs to be those among us who are willing and able to stand up to the powers that benefit so unfairly from the current economic and social arrangements, calling on them to consider the morality of their decisions and to change their relationship to the common good of both humans and Earth. A wonderful new example of this kind of direct action can be found in the Earth Quaker Action Team (EQAT). EQAT has chosen as its target the coal companies and the banks that invest in them, both of which make huge profits from mountaintop removal. Many more such challenges, with many more targets, are likely to be needed in this process of transformation.

We are the Majority

Making the changes that are required to get us to an ecologically integrated economy will require major shifts in consciousness, enormous grassroots mobilization, and taking on the most powerful groups whose interests lie with the status quo. It can seem like an overwhelming task to build an unstoppable national movement of public support for the transformation of our current economic system to one based on ecological integrity. To acknowledge, in the face of multinational corporations and a globalized economy, that this movement must happen on a global level seems even more daunting. Yet, though it may take some time to fully unfold, we can take heart from the fact that this movement has mushroomed worldwide in the last couple of decades.[129] It will help to think of ourselves as the majority:

- All those who quietly resist the lure of advertising;
- Everybody who chooses to act—in their family, their community, their work—as a producer rather than a consumer;
- Every landless person pressing for land reform and access to the resources of his or her home region;
- Every member and potential member of every cooperative enterprise;
- Every person who takes responsibility for their community and works to make it a more flourishing, resilient, and ecologically integrated place to live;
- Every gifted designer or engineer who develops and shares processes that cut down on energy or resource use;
- Every entrepreneur who forsakes profit as the ultimate goal;
- All those groups who toil to move their chosen policy or piece of legislation incrementally forward;
- Everybody who cares about their grandchildren;
- Everybody who cares about Earth; and
- Every person of faith who sees the sacred in our work and our relationship to Earth.

Many people who have never thought of themselves as part of a movement, but who hold these values and work in these ways, are poised to understand that a livable future depends on transformative change at the intersection of economics and ecology. Not only are we the majority, but we have on our side the guidance of both life and truth. Before us is the task to align our lives with that guidance, boldly claim each other and those two great allies—life and truth—and step out into the public arena, speaking up about what we love and what we know.

ENDNOTES

(Full citations are in the Bibliography following. Websites were accessed 12 September 2012 unless otherwise indicated.)

Chapter One "Introduction: The Growth Dilemma Project"

1. Berry (1999)
2. Boulding (1965)
3. Joe Volk often says this, quoting the architect who designed FCNL's green building renovation.
4. Brown *et al* (2009)
5. Growth Dilemma Project <pym.org/committee/ growth-dilemma-project-gdp-pym>.
6. Philadelphia Yearly Meeting of the Religious Society of Friends (1978)
7. Brown (2004)
8. Schellenhuber *et al*, (2004), Costanza *et al* (2007), Sherwood and Huber (2010)
9. Brown and Schmidt (2010)
10. Boulding (1964, 1965, 1966, 1988)
11. Daly (1991, 1994, 1996a)
12. Berry (1999)

Chapter Two "The Growth Dilemma"

13. Boulding (1965)
14. Global Footprint Network world footprint <footprintnetwork.org/en/ index.php/GFN/page/world_footprint>, U.S. footprint <footprintnet-work.org/en/index.php/GFN/page/trends/unitedstate>
15. Millenium Ecosystem Assessment (2005) <maweb.org>
16. Brown *et al* (2009)
17. A more complete description of our current economic system is in the companion volume (QIF #5) to this QIF #6 pamphlet Dreby *et al* (2012), entitled *It's the Economy, Friends: Understanding the Growth Dilemma* (IEF)
18. Dreby (2007), IEF 24-57
19. Kurtzman (1994), Dreby and Helmuth (2002), IEF pp. 47-57
20. IEF pp. 47-57

Chapter Three "Is Good Growth Possible?"

21. Saez and Piketty (2003) and Table A1 in Saez (2007)
22. <reclaimdemocracy.org/corporate_accountability/powell_memo_lewis. html>
23. For detailed explanations, see Khana Academy <khanacademy. org/finance-economics/microeconomics/v/production-possibilities-frontier> or Investopedia <investopedia.com/university/economics/ economics2.asp#axzz26gPlitA6>

Chapter Four "Can Prosperity Continue Without Economic Growth"

24. Ciscel *et al* (2011)
25. Charles A. S. Hall is a former student of Howard T. Odum, and now a researcher in biophysical economics studying world economic growth patterns in relation to energy sources. This line of energy science reasoning began with Frederick Soddy (Daly, 1996), and continued with Kenneth Boulding (1966), and Nicholas Georgescu-Rogen (1971). Howard T. Odum and Betty Odum (2001) published an assessment of

the guidance provided by biophysical economics for the fundamental re-adaptation of human settlements to earth's ecosystems. Herman Daly (2004) draws heavily on biophysical economics.

26. Hall and Klitgaard (2011) <8020vision.com/2011/10/17/energy-return-on-investment-eroi-for-u-s-oil-and-gas-discovery-and-production/> and <ftalphaville.ft.com/blog/2012/05/02/983171/marginal-oil-production-costs-are-heading-towards-100barrel>
27. Heinberg (2012) and Kamm (2012)
28. Diouhy (2012)
29. From a presentation by Charles Hall at the Montreal De-Growth Conference, May 14-20, 2012
30. Hansen (2012)
31. McKibben (2012)
32. Yasuni National Park <sosyasuni.org/en/index.php>
33. Tainter (1990)
34. Beck (1999) and Mythen (2004)
35. Boulding (1965)
36. Hansen (2012) and McKibben (2012).
37. Korten (2010)
38. Ferguson (2012)
39. Martin (2012)
40. There are a lot of people thinking about this and a growing number of books on the theme: Catton (1982), Costa (2010), Coyle (2011), De Villers (2012), Gilding (2011), Heinberg (2011), Homer-Dixon (2006), Jackson (2011), Jones (2008), Lewis and Conaty (2012), Rifkin (2011), Turner (2011), and Victor (2008).
41. Bradford (2006)
42. Cunningham (2002)
43. Hutchinson, Mellor, and Olson (2002)
44. Huber and Robertson (2010), Kucinich (2011), Hallsmith and Lietar (2011)
45. Lewis and Conaty (2012)
46. Rubin (2010). Shipping companies are now attempting to temporarily offset rising oil prices by building even larger container ships that create "economies of scale." The problem is that oil prices will catch up with and wipe out the profitability of these ships as well.

Chapter Five "Meaningful Jobs and Livelihoods"

47. Sahlins (1972)
48. Childe (1950)
49. U.S. Census Bureau, 2010 Census of Labor Force, Employment, and Earnings – Employed Persons dataset 616, <census.gov/compendia/statab/2012/tables/12s0616.xls> Accessed June 26, 2012
50. Estimated U. S. Unemployment rate from 1890-2011. 1890–1930 data are from Romer (1986). 1930–1940 data are from Coen (1973). 1940–2011 data are from Bureau of Labor Statistics. Bureau of Labor Statistics, Employment status of the civilian non-institutional population, 1940 to date. Retrieved March 6, 2009, and Historical Comparability (2006). Employment and Earnings. Household Data Explanatory Notes, February 2006 <bls.gov/cps/eetech_methods.pdf>
51. U.S. Bureau of Labor Statistics – Economic New Release: Employment Status of ... 16-24 Years of Age, <bls. gov/news. release/youth. t01. htm> Accessed June 29, 2012.
52. Williams (2012)
53. Braungart (2002)

54. Medscape web site. <medscape.com/features/slideshow/
compensation/2012/public?src=google&ef_id=BW9P-
HPLJnMAAB@X:20120809140022:s> Accessed August 9, 2012 and
<data.bls.gov/timeseries/LNS14000000>
55. <timebanks.org>
56. <ithacahours.org> accessed on August 25, 2012
57. <berkshares. org/press/index. Htm> Accessed on August 25, 2012.
58. Thomas Paine, "Agrarian Justice" <geolib. com/essays/paine. tom/
agjst.html> Accessed on August 25, 2012.
59. Ravetnos (2007)
60. Ackerman and Alstott (1999)

Chapter Six "Establishing Responsible Production"

61. Haines (2004)
62. Korten (2010) p. 28
63. Korten (2001) and Ritz (2001)
64. Friedman (1970)
65. Shuman (2012), p.45
66. Bruyn (1980)
67. IEF pp. 1–2
68. IEF pp. 2–8
69. Bruyn (1980)
70. Heinberg (2011)
71. Franklin (1999) p. 79 and following pp.
72. Knowlton (2007) and Zero Emissions Research & Initiatives <seri.
org>, a global network with a common vision of viewing waste as
resource and seeking solutions using nature's design principles as
inspiration.
73. <designboom.com/eng/funclub/cradle.html> retrieved June 1, 2012
74. <yesmagazine.org/people-power/pittsburg-bans-natural-gas-drilling>
75. <guardian.co.uk/environment/2011/apr/10/
bolivia-enshrines-natural-worlds-rights>
76. <yesmagazine.org/blogs/sarah-van-gelder/
dear-big-coal-youre-not-above-the-law>
77. <bmu.de/english/waste_management/general_information/doc/4304.
php> and <eprworkinggroup.org>
78. <campaignlive.co.uk/news/575994>

Chapter Seven "The Commons, Collaborative Organizations"

79. Hardin (1968)
80. Ostrom's work has been reviewed in detail in a previous pamphlet
(QIF #2) in this series, Ciscel, Day, Helmth, Lewis, and Lumb (2011)
*How on Earth Do We Live Now: Natural Capital, Deep Ecology, and
the Commons.*
81. Ostrom (1990)
82. Ciscel *et al* (2011)
83. <fourthsector.net>
84. <chaordicinitiatives.org>
85. <is4ie.org>
86. Barnes (2006)
87. <nhtinc.org/ice.php>
88. Barnes (2006)
89. Wilkerson and Pickett (2009)
90. Steele (2012)

91. *ibid.*
92. Russell (2000)
93. <noosphere.org>
94. <blogs.opentext.com/vca/blog/1.11.512/article/1.26.1103/2011/8/31/ Here_Comes_Web_4.0> and <pcworld.com/article/143110/article. html>
95. <panarchy.org>
96. Benker (2006)
97. Rifkin (2009)
98. *ibid.*
99. Rifkin (2011)
100. Fuller (1968)
101. Daly (1973)
102. Hawken *et al* (2008)
103. von Weizsacker *et al* (2009)
104. <cooperationcommons.com>
105. Hawken (2008)
106. Laszlo and Dennis (2012)

Chapter Eight "An Ecologically Integrated Economy

107. Boulding (1965)
108. Daly (1973)
109. Boulding (1965)
110. Hawken *et al* (2008) and IEF pp. 27-28
111. Daly and Farley (2004) Chapters 5 and 6
112. Daly and Cobb (1994) This quotation appears in their Afterward on "Money, Debt and Wealth."
113. Henry Ford <quotes4all.net/quote_1477.html>
114. <monetary.org>, <en.wikipedia.org/wiki/A_Program_for_Monetary_ Reform>, and <youtube.com/watch?v=0CaYuss28HQ>
115. Friend Paul Krumm has an unpublished article, "The Values of Money," which addresses many of these issues that he will provide electronically on request <phkrumm@rhelectric.net>.
116. Rokeach (1973)
117. Asimov (1974)
118. Bouldling (1964)
119. Kennedy (1995)
120. Chang (2008) Chapter 9
121. The work of three Friends bears directly on this issue: David George (in press), Edward Morgan (2010), and David C. McClelland (1975)
122. Boulding (1965)
123. Boulding (1964)
124. Vaclav Haval <http://thinkexist.com/quotation/hope_is_not_the_con- viction_that_something_will/177680.html>
125. Joe Volk, Commencement Address at Wilmington College <fcnl.org/ about/who/staff/writings/practicing_hope_way_opens/>
126. John C. Cobb, personal communication, February 10, 2011

Chapter Nine "The Way Forward"

127. The Inclusive Prosperity Act (HR 6311) was introduced in the 112th Congress, U.S. House of Representatives <robinhoodtax.org>.
128. The National Emergency Employment Defense Act (HR 2990) was introduced September 21st of 2011 <monetary.org>.
129. Hawken (2007)

BIBLIOGRAPHY

Ackerman, Bruce, and Anne Alstott, 1999. *The Stakeholder Society.* New Haven CN: Yale University Press.

Asimov, Isaac, 1974. *Earth Our Crowded Spaceship*, New York NY: John Day (published in cooperation with UNICEF for World Population Year).

Barnes, Peter, 2006. *Capitalism 3.0: A Guide to Reclaiming the Commons.* San Francisco CA: Berrett-Koehler.

Beck, Ulrich, 1999. *World Risk Society.* Cambridge UK: Polity Press.

Benker, Yochai, 2006. *The Wealth of Networks: How Social Production Transforms Markets and Freedom.* New Haven CN: Yale University Press. <jus.uio.no/sisu/the_wealth_of_networks.yochai_benkler/book_index.html>.

Berry, Thomas, 1999. *The Great Work: Our Way Into the Future.* New York NY: Bell Tower/Random House.

Boulding, Kenneth, 1964. *The Meaning of the 20th Century: The Great Transition.* New York: Harper and Row, Publishers.

Boulding, Kenneth, 1965. Earth as a Spaceship <quakerinstitute.org/?page_id=482>.

Boulding, Kenneth, 1964. *The Meaning of the 20th Century.* Originally published by Harper and Row and reprinted in 1988 by Lanham MD: University Press of America.

Boulding, Kenneth, 1966. The Economics of the Coming Spaceship Earth. In *Environmental Quality in a Growing Economy,* H. Jarrett, Ed. Washington DC: RFF Press.

Boulding, Kenneth, 1970. *Economics as a Science.* Originally published by McGraw-Hill and reprinted in 1988 by Lanham MD: University Press of America.

Bradford, Travis, 2006. *Solar Revolution: The Economic Transformation of the Global Energy Industry.* Cambridge MA: MIT Press.

Braungart, Michael, 2002. *Cradle to Cradle: Remaking the Way We Make Things.* New York NY: North Point Press.

Brown, Lester, 2004. *Outgrowing the Earth.* New York: W.W. Norton.

Brown, Peter G., Geoffrey Garver, Keith Helmuth, Robert Howell, Steve Szeghi, 2009. *Right Relationship: Building a Whole Earth Economy.* San Francisco CA: Berrett-Koehler Publishers.

Brown, Peter G. and Jeremy J. Schmidt, 2010. An Ethic of Compassionate Retreat. In *Water Ethics: Foundational Readings for Students and Professionals,* Peter G. Brown and Jeremy J. Schmidt, Eds. Washington DC: Island Press. <humansandnature.org/an-ethic-of-compassionate-retreat-article-102.php>

Bruyn, Severyn, 1980. *Quaker Testimonies and Economic Alternatives*, Wallingford PA: Pendle Hill Pamphlet #231.

Catton, William R., 1982. *Overshoot: The Ecological Basis of Revolutionary Change*. Urbana IL: University of Illinois Press.

Chang, Ha-Joon, 2008. *Bad Samaritans: The Myth of Free Trade and the Secret History of Capitalism*. New York NY: Bloomsbury Press.

Childe, V. Gordon, 1950. The Urban Revolution. *Town Planning Review* 21 (1) 3-17 (April 1950).

Ciscel, David, Barbara Day, Keith Helmuth, Sandra Lewis, and Judy Lumb, 2011. *How on Earth Do We Live Now? Natural Capital, Deep Ecology, and the Commons.* Quaker Institute for the Future Pamphlet #2, Caye Caulker, Belize: *Producciones de la Hamaca.*

Coen, Robert M. , 1973. Labor Force and Unemployment in the 1920s and 1930s: A Re-Examination Based on Postwar Experience. *The Review of Economics and Statistics,* 55(1): 46–55.

Costanza, Robert, Lisa Graumlich, Will Steffen, Eds., 2007. *Sustainability or Collapse: An Integrated History and Future of People on Earth.* Cambridge MA: MIT Press.

Costa, Rebecca D., 2010. *The Watchman's Rattle: Thinking Our Way Out of Extinction.* Philadelphia PA: Vanguard.

Coyle, Diane, 2011. *The Economics of Enough: How to Run the Economy as if the Future Matters.* Princeton NJ: Princeton University Press.

Cunningham, Storm, 2002. *The Restoration Economy: Immediate & Emerging Opportunities for Businesses, Communities, and Investors.* San Francisco CA: Berrett-Koehler.

Daly, Herman E., 1973. *Steady-State Economics,* 1st Edition. New York NY: W. H. Freeman.

Daly, Herman E., 1991. *Steady-State Economics,* 2nd Edition. Washington DC: Island Press.

Daly, Herman E. 1996a. *Beyond Growth: The Economics of Sustainable Development.* Boston: Beacon Press.

Daly, Herman E. 1996b. The Economic Thought of Frederick Soddy. *Beyond Growth: The Economics of Sustainable Development.* Boston: Beacon Press <nytimes.com/2009/04/12/opinion/12zencey. html?pagewanted=all>.

Daly, Herman E., 1996c. On Nicholas Georgescu-Rogen's Contribution to Economics. *Beyond Growth: The Economics of Sustainable Development.* Boston: Beacon Press.

Daly, Herman E. and John B. Cobb, Jr. 1994. *For the Common Good: Redirecting the Economy Toward Community, the Environment, and a Sustainable Future,* 2nd Edition. Boston: Beacon Press.

Daly, Herman E. and Joshua Farley, 2004. *Ecological Economics: Principles and Applications.* Washington DC: Island Press.

De Villers, Marq, 2012. *Our Way Out: First Principles for a Post-Apocalyptic World.* New York NY: Random House.

Dietz, Rob, and Dan O'Neill, 2012. *Enough is Enough: Building a Sustainable Economy in a World of Finite Resources.* San Francisco CA: Berrett-Koehler Publishers.

Diouhy, Jennifer, 2012. *Administration touts 'Great Green Fleet' test exercises with biofuels* <fuelfix.com/blog/2012/07/20/administration -touts-great-green-fleet-test-exercises-with- biofuels>.

Dreby, Ed, 2007. Money and Growth: Another Inconvenient Truth? *Quaker Eco-Bulletin* 7:2.

Dreby, Ed, 2011. The Growth Dilemma: Understanding the Need for Change. *Quaker Eco-Bulletin* 11:2.

Dreby, Ed and Keith Helmuth, 2002. The Financial Economy and the Earth's Ecosystems: A Primer. *Quaker Eco-Bulletin* 2:4.

Dreby, Ed, Keith Helmuth, Margaret Mansfield, 2012. *It's the Economy, Friends: Understanding the Growth Dilemma.* Quaker Institute for the Future pamphlet #5. Caye Caulker: *Producciones de la Hamaca.* <quakerinstitute.org/wp-content/uploads/2012/06/ IEF-web.pdf>.

Ferguson, Charles, 2012. *Predator Nation: Corporate Criminals, Political Corruption, and the Hijacking of America,* New York NY: Random House.

Franklin, Ursula, 1999. *The Real World of Technology.* House of Anansi.

Friedman, Milton, 1970. The Social Responsibility of Business is to Increase its Profits, *New York Times Magazine,* September 13, 1970.

George, David, 2004. *Preference Pollution: How Markets Create the Desires We Dislike (Economics, Cognition, and Society).* Ann Arbor MI: University of Michigan Press.

George, David, (in press) *The Rhetoric of the Right: Language Change and the Spread of the Market.* Abingdon, Oxon, UK: Routledge Press.

Georgescu-Rogen, Nicholas, 1971. *The Entropy Law and Economic Process.* Cambridge MA: Harvard University Press.

Gilding, Paul, 2011. *The Great Disruption: Why Climate the Change Crisis Will Bring on the End of Shopping and the Birth of a New World.* New York NY: Bloomsbury.

Haines, Walter, (2004). A Correspondence on Economics, *Friends Journal,* December 2004.

Hall, Charles A. S. and Kent Klitgaard, 2011. *Energy and the Wealth of Nations: Understanding the Biophysical Economy.* Secaucus NJ: Springer <esf.edu/EFB/hall/>.

Hallsmith, Gwendolyn and Bernard Lietar, 2011. *Creating Wealth: Growing Local Economies with Local Currencies.* Gabriola Island BC: New Society Publishers.

Hansen, James, 2012. Game Over for the Climate *New York Times,* May10, 2012   <nytimes.com/2012/05/10/opinion/game-over-for-the-climate. html>.

Hardin, Garrett, 1968. The Tragedy of the Commons. *Science* 280 (5364): 682-3 *<sciencemag.org/content/162/3859/1243.full>*.

Hawken, Paul, Amory Lovins, and L. Hunter Lovins, 2008. *Natural Capitalism: Creating the Next Industrial Revolution.* New York NY: Back Bay Books/Little, Brown & Co.

Hawken, Paul, 2008. *Blessed Unrest: How the Largest Social Movement in History Is Restoring Grace, Justice, and Beauty to the World.* New York NY: Penguin Books.

Heinberg, Richard, 2011. *The End of Growth: Adapting to Our New Economic Reality.* Gabriola Island BC: New Society Publishers. <energybulleting.net/stories/2011-03-16/earth-limits-why-growth-wont-return-metals-and-other minerals>.

Heinberg, Richard, 2012. Don't Worry, There's Plenty of Oil. <postcarbon. org/blog-post/1083449-don-t-worry-there-s-plenty-of-oil>.

Homer-Dixon, Thomas, 2006. *The Upside of Down: Catastrophe, Creativity, and the Renewal of Civilization.* Washington DC: Island Press.

Huber and Robertson, 2010. *Creating New Money: A Monetary Reform for the Information Age.* London: New Economics Foundation <jamesrobertson.com/book/creatingnewmoney.pdf>.

Hutchinson, Francis, Mary Mellor, and Wendy Olson, 2002. *The Politics of Money: Towards Sustainability and Economic Democracy.* London: Pluto Press.

Jackson, Tim, 2011. *Prosperity Without Growth: Economics for a Finite Planet.* London: Earthscan.

Jacobs, Jane, 1984. *Cities and the Wealth of Nations: Principles of Economic Life.* New York NY: Random House.

Jones, Van, 2008. *The Green Collar Economy: How One Solution Can Fix our Two Biggest Problems.* New York NY: HarperCollins Publishers.

Kamm, David, 2012. Energy Expert Says Oil Production Has Peaked. <news-press.com/article/20120826/BUSINESS/308260019/Energy-expert-says- world-s-oil-production-has-peaked?odyssey=mod|news well|text|Home|s>.

Kennedy, Margrit, and Susan Meeker-Lowry, 1995. *Interest and Inflation-Free Money, Creating an Exchange Medium that Works for Everybody and Protects the Earth.* Gabriola Island BC: New Society Publishers.

Knowlton, Hollister, 2007 ZERI: A Philosophy and Methodology to Reinvent the World, *Quaker Eco-Bulletin* 7:6.

Korten, David C., 2001. *When Corporations Rule the World*. San Francisco CA: Berrett-Koehler Publishers.

Korten, David C., 2010. *Agenda for a New Economy: From Phantom Wealth to Real Wealth,* 2nd Edition. San Francisco CA: Berrett-Koehler.

Kucinich, Dennis, 2011. House of Representatives Bill 2990, 2011.<monetary.org/wp-content/uploads/2011/11/HR-2990.pdf>

Kurtzman, Joel, 1994. *The Death of Money: How the Electronic Economy Has Destablized the World's Markets and Created Financial Chaos.* New York NY: Little Brown & Co.

Laszlo, Ervin, and Kingsley L. Dennis, 2012. *The New Science and Spirituality Reader*. New York NY: Inner Traditions/Bear & Company.

Lewis, Michael and Pat Conaty, 2012. *The Resilience Imperative: Cooperative Transitions To a Steady-State Economy*. Gabriola Island BC: New Society Publishers.

Lietaer, Bernard and Stephen Belgin, 2011. *New Money for a New World*. Denver CO: QiterraPress <newmoneyforanewworld.com>.

Martin, Patrick, 2012. Consumer Slowdown Hits U.S. Economy. <wsws.org/articles/2012/jul2012/econ-j28.shtml>.

McClelland, David C., 1975. *Power: The Inner Experience*. New York NY: Irvington/Halsted.

McKibben, Bill, 2012. What NASA's Blue Marble Photo Reveals about Climate Change. *Mother Jones*, February 8, 2012 <motherjones.com/environment/2012/02/bill-mckibben-nasa-blue-marble-photo-climate-change>. .

Meadows, Donella, Jorgen Randers, Dennis Meadows, 2004. *Limits to Growth: The 30-Year Update*. White River Junction VT: Chelsea Green.

Millennium Ecosystem Assessment, 2005. *Ecosystems and Human Well-being: Synthesis*. Washington, DC: Island Press.

Morgan, Edward, 2010. *What Really Happened to the 1960s: How Mass Media Culture Failed American Democracy*. Lawrence KS: University Press of Kansas.

Mythen, Gabe, 2004. *Ulrich Beck: A Critical Introduction to the Risk Society*. London: Pluto Press.

Odum, Howard T. and Betty Odum, 2001. *A Prosperous Way Down: Principles and Policies*. Boulder CO: University Press of Colorado <emergysociety.org>.

Ostrom, Elinor, 1990. *Governing the Commons: The Evolution of Institutions for Collective Action*. New York NY: Cambridge University Press.

Paine, Thomas, 1987. *The Thomas Paine Reader*. New York: Penguin Classics.

Philadelphia Yearly Meeting of the Religious Society of Friends, 1978. *Faith and Practice*. Philadelphia: Philadelphia Yearly Meeting.

Polanyi, Karl, 1968. *Primitive, Archaic and Modern Economies: Essays of Karl Polanyi*, Edited by George Dalton. Garden City NY: Anchor Books, Doubleday and Company.

Ravetnos, Daniel, 2007. *Basic Income: The Material Conditions of Freedom*. London: Pluto Press <basicincome. org/bien>.

Rifkin, Jeremy, 2009. *The Empathic Civilization: The Race to Global Consciousness in a World in Crisis*. New York NY: Jeremy P. Tarcher/ Penguin Books.

Rifkin, Jeremy, 2011. *The Third Industrial Revolution: How Lateral Power is Transforming Energy, the Economy, and the World*. New York: Palgrave Macmillan.

Ritz, Dean, ed., 2001. *Defying Corporations, Defining Democracy*. Lanham MD: Marylan Apex Press/Rowman and Littlefield.

Rokeach, Milton, 1973. The Nature of Human Values. New York NY: The Free Press.

Romer, Christina (1986). Spurious Volatility in Historical Unemployment Data. *The Journal of Political Economy,* 94(1): 1–37.

Rubin, Jeff, 2010; *Why Your World Is About To Get A Whole Lot Smaller*. New York: Random House.

Russell, Peter, 2000. *The Global Brain Awakens: Our Next Evolutionary Leap*. Tisbury, Wiltshire, England: Element Books.

Saez, Emmanuel, 2007. Table A1: Top fractiles income shares (excluding capital gains) in the U.S., 1913–2005, data provided by the Econometrics Laboratory Software Archive <elsa.berkeley.edu/~saez/ TabFig2005prel.xls>.

Saez, Emmanuel and Thomas Piketty, 2003. Income inequality in the United States: 1913–1998. *Quarterly Journal of Economics*, 118(1), 1–39.

Sahlins, Marshall D., 1972. *Stone Age Economics*. Hawthorne NY: Aldine de Gruyter, Inc. pp. 17-24.

Schellenhuber, Hans, Paul Crutzen, William C. Clark, Martin Claussen, Hermann Held, Eds., 2004. *Earth System Analysis for Sustainability*. Cambridge MA: MIT Press.

Sherwood, S. and Huber, M., 2010. An Adaptability Limit to Climate Change Due to Heat Stress. *Proc. Nat'l. Acad. Sciences*, v. 107 (21), pp. 9552-9555.

Shuman, Michael, 2012. *Local Dollars, Local Sense: How to Shift Your Money from Wall Street to Main Street and Achieve Real Prosperity--A*

Community Resilience Guide. White River Junction VT: Chelsea Green Publishing.

Simms, Andrew, 2005. *Ecological Debt: The Health of the Planet and the Wealth of Nations.* London: Pluto Press.

Steele, Robert David, 2012. *The Open-Source Everything Manifesto: Transparency, Truth, and Trust.* New York NY: Evolver Editions/ Random House.

Stilgoe, John R., 1998. *Outside Lies Magic: Regaining History and Awareness in Everyday Places.* New York NY: Walker and Company.

Stone, Christopher D., 2010. *Should Trees Have Standing? Law, Morality, and the Environment,* 3rd edition. New York NY: Oxford University Press.

Tainter, Joseph, 1990. *The Collapse of Complex Societies.* New York NY: Cambridge University Press.

Turner, Chris, 2011. *The Leap: How to Survive and Thrive in the Sustainable Economy.* New York NY: Random House.

Victor, Peter, 2008. *Managing Without Growth: Slower by Design, Not Disaster.* Cheltenham UK: Edward Elgar.

Waring, M. 1988. *Counting for Nothing: What Men Value and What Women are Worth.* Reprinted in 1996 by Welllington, New Zealand: Bridget Williams Books.

von Weizsacker, Ernst Ulrich, Charlie Hargroves, Michael H. Smith, Cheryl Desha, Peter Stasinopoulos, 2009. *Factor Five: Transforming the Global Economy through 80% Improvements in Resource Productivity.* Florence KY: Routledge/Taylor & Francis.

Williams, John, 2012. Shadow Government Statistics – Analysis Behind and Beyond Government Economic Reporting. <shadowstats.com/ alternate_data/unemployment-charts> Accessed on 6/29/2012.

Wilkerson, Richard and Kate Pickett, 2009. *The Spirit Level: Why Equality is Better for Everyone.* Washington DC: Penguin Books <equalitytrust. org.uk>.

Wood, Ellen Meiksins, 2002. *The Origin of Capitalism: A Longer View.* London: Verso.

Zero Emissions Research and Initiatives <zeri.org>.

DISCUSSION QUESTIONS
It's the Economy, Friends (IEF) Chapter One
1. What can we learn that applies to our current problems from early Quakers such as John Bellers, William Penn, and John Woolman?

2. How does Kenneth Boulding's concept of a spaceship economy in contrast to a cowboy economy apply today in our economic system?

3. What do you see as the biggest problems of the new millennium, how do they impact your life, and what are Quakers doing to address them?

IEF Chapter Two
4. What do you understand about markets, how their functioning has evolved to our current economic system, and how they relate to our daily lives?

5. How do you see orthodox economics and/or ecological economics fitting with Quaker values and testimonies?

6. What do you understand about the basic economics concepts of negative externalities and cost-benefit analysis? How do they play out in your own life and decision making?

7. Does the combination of natural capital, human capital, social capital and physical capital adequately capture the total of our wealth?

8. What do you understand about money, how it is created and managed? What is the role of fractional reserve banking and interest in driving economic growth? What is your relationship with money?

IEF Chapter Three
9. Do you know of unintended consequences that have occurred with economic policy interventions? How are positive and negative feedbacks working in our modern industrial economy?

10. How well does the current economic system value people and nature? How equally is the wealth shared? Are there better alternatives? Does the model for managing the economy offered by ecological economists seem workable?

11. Where do you see structural violence in the economic system, and in your own life?

12. Is our testimony of simplicity adequate to address the structural violence in the world? If not, what more is needed?

13. What can we learn from other nations' approach to eliminating poverty, managing fossil fuel reserves, and addressing financial collapse?

14. What are the most significant differences between corporations and cooperatives or other alternatives to publicly traded corporations? What is your experience of these differences? What guidance about corporate reform can we glean from Quaker values?

15. What seem to be the major drivers of both natural and economic growth? What seem to be the most compelling limits to both natural and economic growth? How do the Quaker testimonies guide us to address the issue of economic growth?

Beyond the Growth Dilemma (BGD) Chapter One

16. What gives a person integrity? What might give an economy integrity? What is the role of the economy in our lives?

BGD Chapter Two

17. What is attractive about a "cowboy economy" that might make it hard to shift to a "spaceship economy"?

18. What can grow indefinitely without negative consequences and what kinds of growth need limits?

BGD Chapter Three

19. What are some of the problems of our economy today? What are some solutions?

20. How can the full cost of a product be captured in its price?

BGD Chapter Four

21. What needs to grow, what needs to subside, and what needs to stay steady in our economic system?

22. How can we shift the general attitude that "more is better" to one based upon "enough"?

BGD Chapter Five

23. What are some ways that you find credible to address the problem of high unemployment?

24. To what kinds of livelihood or mix of work would we want our children and grandchildren to aspire? How could they gain the skills and knowledge they will need?

25. What kind of income security would provide a safety net without discouraging personal initiative?

BGC Chapter Six

26. What would have to shift for our economic system to focus on producing goods and services that improve our lives, rather than creating and filling "needs" for consumer goods?

27. How can the power of the private sector and the power of government best be balanced? What needs to happen to regain that balance?

28. What will encourage production to shift from linear to circular models?

29. How will the growing importance of recyclability, durability, reparability, and service affect technology, production, and economic priorities?

30. How can an appropriate mix of taxation, subsidy and regulation be developed to ensure responsible production in a democratic society? What are the basic principles?

31. What rights does or should nature have?

BGD Chapter Seven

32. How might the commons best be governed?

33. What are the potentials of emerging communications and networking technologies?

34. We used to see resources as abundant and human labor as the limiting factor. What are the implications of that relationship being reversed?

BGD Chapter Eight

35. What must we give up to keep what we value most?

36. What area some equitable and respectful ways to address the issue of population growth?

37. What feedback mechanisms are needed to create and maintain an ecologically integrated economy?

BGD Chapter Nine

38. What is a healthy mix between action on an individual, community and national scale? Is there something that everybody should be doing on each level?

39. How do we decide on which national legislation to focus our energies? What are the guiding principles?

40. What gives us hope?

Contributors

Ed Dreby is a retired social studies teacher and secondary school administrator. He is the project leader of the Growth Dilemma Project.

Pamela Haines is the public policy director of an early childhood organization, writes and leads workshops on faith and economics, and clerks the Growth Dilemma Project.

Keith Helmuth has been a small business entrepreneur and community development activist. He is the Secretary of the Board of Trustees of the Quaker Institute for the Future.

Stephen Loughin teaches physics at St. Joseph's University (PA). He is also a consultant on waste minimization strategies for material suppliers and provides technology support to a reading and literacy company he helped start in 1998. He is a member of the Growth Dilemma Project.

Judy Lumb is the publishing agent for Quaker Institute for the Future through her publishing non-governmental organization, *Producciones de la Hamaca* in Caye Caulker, Belize. She is on the editorial teams for *What Canst Thou Say?* and *Quaker Eco-Bulletin*.

J. Tucker Taylor is an economist teaching at Temple University in Philadelphia. He has worked on economic development projects in North, West and East Africa, and in American inner cities. His interests include macroeconomic policy and labor markets, in particular how to get our unemployment rate down to some sustainable, but more importantly just, humane minimum.

David Watkins is retired from federal service. He grew up on a farm, worked in the private sector from small businesses to large corporations, worked for government at the city, county, state and federal levels, and served as a volunteer for several civic organizations. For over 40 years he has been an advocate of a comprehensive and whole systems approach.

QUAKER INSTITUTE FOR THE FUTURE

Advancing a global future of inclusion, social justice, and ecological integrity through participatory research and discernment.

The Quaker Institute for the Future (QIF) seeks to generate systematic insight, knowledge, and wisdom that can inform public policy and enable us to treat all humans, all communities of life, and the whole Earth as manifestations of the Divine. QIF creates the opportunity for Quaker scholars and practitioners to apply the social and ecological intelligence of their disciplines within the context of Friends' testimonies and the Quaker traditions of truth seeking and public service.

The focus of the Institute's concerns include:

- Economic behavior that increasingly undermines the ecological processes on which life depends.

- The development of technologies and capabilities that hold us responsible for the future of humanity and the Earth.

- Structural violence and lethal conflict arising from the pressures of change, increasing inequity, concentrations of power and wealth, declining natural capital, and increasing militarism.

- The increasing separation of people into areas of poverty and wealth, and into social domains of aggrandizement and deprivation.

- The philosophy of individualism and its socially corrosive promotion as the principal means for the achievement of the common good.

- The complexity of global interdependence and its demands on governance systems and citizen's responsibilities.

- The convergence of ecological and economic breakdown into societal disintegration.

<quakerinstitute.org>

CPSIA information can be obtained at www.ICGtesting.com
Printed in the USA
BVOW012329081112

305062BV00001B/5/P